RIGHTS OF WAY

Footpaths and Bridleways

by

Simon Blackford
MA, Barrister

Barnards Inn Chambers

CLT PROFESSIONAL PUBLISHING
A DIVISION OF CENTRAL LAW TRAINING LTD

© **Simon Blackford** 1995

Published by
CLT Professional Publishing
A Division of Central Law Training Ltd
Wrens Court
52-54 Victoria Road
Sutton Coldfield
Birmingham B72 1SX

ISBN 1 85811 055 6

Typeset by Cheryl Zimmerman
Printed in Great Britain by The Lavenham Press Ltd

RIGHTS

OF

WAY

Footpaths and Bridleways

Contents

Preface

Almost all of us use highways every day of our lives. But unlike the law that governs our other everyday affairs – contract, tort, employment, family – highway law is for some reason regarded as obscure and beyond the reach of most students and dabblers.

Although not all of us use footpaths and bridleways every day, walking in the countryside is a hugely popular recreational activity. To many of those walkers the extent and limitation of their rights are by no means obvious. Even if they are a good deal better at reading maps than I am, it can be daunting to be confronted by a field with no way marked across it, however sure they may be that a right of way exists. Whilst this book will be of limited assistance as they stand on the edge of the field contemplating their predicament, it may help them to get something done about the situation so that they and others will not suffer the same difficulty in the future. I hope that this book may provide a useful and not too obscure source of information to such users of footpaths and bridleways as well as being of more comprehensive use to those who are professionally involved with rights of way.

I would like to thank Mr James Richardson, senior solicitor, of Kent County Council for the information he helpfully provided regarding footpath inquiries.

The law is stated as at 1 September 1995.

Simon Blackford

Table of Cases

TABLE OF CASES

Table of Statutes

CHAPTER 1

Introduction

Introduction

The labyrinth of footpaths and bridleways in England and Wales, stretching over 100,000 miles, is a huge recreational asset. But only 100 years ago substantially the same labyrinth was more functional than recreational. Before the advent of the motor car footpaths and bridleways were a vital means of getting to work, visiting relatives and friends and so on. Today most such journeys are undertaken by motor transport, whether public or private. As with the canals, a system which had a vital ecomomic and social value now has a very high recreational value.

This radical change in the way we use footpaths and bridleways has coloured not only our way of seeing footpaths and bridleways but even the language and concepts we use. No doubt 100 years ago the word "highway" conjured up various forms of way, including footpaths and bridleways as well as rural carriage ways and urban streets. Indeed there may not have been a very great difference between a minor rural road which served as a carriageway and some bridleways and footpaths. Today to many people the term "highway" immediately brings to mind a metalled road which is made to accommodate motor vehicles and bears little resemblance to a footpath across a field.

The preservation of the network of footpaths and bridleways has been facilitated by statutory measures. Whilst it has for a very long time been the rule that "once a highway always a highway", the infrequent use of many footpath and bridleways would undoubtedly have resulted in the loss of many had it not been for the introduction of the definitive map which highway authorities are now required to keep.

Common Law and Statute Law

The law of footpaths and bridleways is now largely to be found in a comprehensive and detailed statutory framework. A great deal of this framework is contained in the *Highways Act 1980*. Other provisions are contained in the *Countryside Act 1968*, the *Wildlife and Countryside Act 1981*, the *Rights of Way Act 1990* and various other statutes and statutory instruments. However there is still a core of common law decisions which lies at the centre of the law which is very important to a correct understanding of the law of highways including the statutory framework. To take one important example, the term "highway" is not defined in the Highways Act whereas an understanding of the term is vital to a proper understanding of the Act.

One feature of this development of the law and the change in the physical network of highways is that there are many statutory provisions which apply to highways (and therefore to footpath and bridleways) which are in effect only applicable to carriageways. A comprehensive statement of the law of footpath and bridleways would therefore contain a good deal of material which is of only nominal relevance. In this book an effort has been made to leave such measures out even though it is not always clear how relevant to footpath and bridleways a measure might be.

The object of this book is to provide an introductory guide to the law relating to footpaths and bridleways.

Meaning of Terms

It is important to define the terms used in this book at an early stage, and indeed an understanding of the meaning of the terms involved in this area of the law itself gives a good deal of insight into the way in which the law operates. The definitions given below are largely taken from the Highways Act 1980. Most of the definitions are to be found in sections 328 and 329 of the Act. Where there is a departure from the Act, it will be made clear. Since so much of the law relating to footpath and bridleways is contained in the Highways Act 1980 ("the Highways Act" – where there is a reference to a previous Highways Act, the year of the Act will be given), these definitions are generally the most important definitions available and as a result are used in contexts outside the scope of the Act. However they are not always the only definitions, so when dealing with an aspect of highway law outside the scope of the Act, the possible divergences have to be borne in mind. Some of the terms defined here concern types of highway which are outside the scope of this book but the meanings are given here to show how footpath and bridleways fit in with the overall system of highways.

Footpath
A highway over which the public have a right of way on foot only, not being a footway.

Bridleway

A right of way for the public on foot or on horse. The full definition in the Highways Act 1980 is "a highway over which the public have the following, but no other, rights of way, that is to say, a right of way on foot and a right of way on horseback or leading a horse, with or without a right to drive animals of any description along the highway."

In addition to rights on foot and on horseback, by section 30 of the Countryside Act 1968 "any member of the public shall have as a right of way the right to ride a bicycle, not being a motor vehicle, on any bridleway, but in exercising this right cyclists shall give way to pedestrians and persons on horseback."

Highway

A common route, which all persons can use to pass and repass along as often as they wish without let or hindrance and without charge. (This is a common law definition. The Highways Act says only: "in this Act except where the context otherwise requires, 'highway' means the whole or part of a highway other than a ferry or a waterway".)

Bridge

For the purposes of the Highways Act 1980, "'Bridge' does not include a culvert, but, save as aforesaid, means a bridge or viaduct which is part of a highway, and includes the abutments and any other part of a bridge but not the highway carried thereby." Additionally, "where a highway passes over a bridge or through a tunnel that bridge or tunnel is to be taken for the purposes of this Act to be part of the highway."

Byway open to all traffic

This term appears in the Wildlife and Countryside Act 1981. It means a highway over which the public have a right of way for vehicular and all other kinds of traffic but which is used by the public mainly for the purposes for which footpaths and bridleways are so used.

Carriageway

"A way constituting or comprised in a highway, being a way (other than a cycle track) over which the public have a right of way for the passage of vehicles."

Cycle track

"A way constituting or comprised in a highway being a way over which the public have the following but no other rights of way, that is to say, a right of way on pedal cycles (other than pedal cycles which are motor vehicles within the meaning of the Road Traffic Act 1972) with or without a right of way on foot."

Definitive map

A map showing all the footpaths and bridleways in a county, together with an accompanying statement concerning such matters as width, limitations on rights, etc. This definitive map is required to be kept in each county. Inclusion in the map is conclusive proof of the existence of the existence of the path and of the rights in question. (Exclusion from the map, however, is not proof that a path or way does not exist.)

Footway

A way comprised in highway which also comprises a carriageway being a way over which the public have a right of way on foot only: a footway is typically a pavement or a path alongside a carriageway. The terms "Footpath" and "Footway" are mutually exclusive.

Highway authority

There are two levels of highway authorities. The Secretary of State is the highway authority for motorways and trunk roads; and the County Councils, the London Boroughs and the Common Council of the City of London, are the local highway authorities which are responsible for other highways. Although the Secretary of State may be the highway authority for a comparatively small number of footpaths and bridleways, the local highway authorities are the highway authority for the vast majority of paths and ways and for the purposes of this book "the highway authority" will mean the local highway authority unless otherwise indicated.

Highway maintainable at the pubic expense

A highway which by virtue of section 36 of the Highways Act 1980 or of any other enactment (whether contained in the Highways Act or not) is a highway which for the purposes of the Act is a highway maintainable at the public expense.

Section 36 states: "all such highways as immediately before the commencement of this Act were maintainable at the public expense for the purposes of the Highways Act 1959 continue to be so maintainable (subject to this section and to any order of a magistrates' court under section 47 below) for the purposes of this Act."

Highways maintainable at the public expense are therefore the following:

- any highway in existence before 31 August 1835;
- streets, roads, paths or ways which came into existence after that date where it can be shown that they have been either adopted or maintained at the public expense at some time since as a highway;
- any highway constructed by the Secretary of State for Transport or a local highway authority;
- highways constructed by local councils and housing action trusts under Housing Act powers where construction has been carried out to the satisfaction of a local highway authority;
- a highway built and dedicated under an agreement between the highway authority and the builder under section 38 of the 1980 Highways Act 1980 or under the Highways Act 1959;
- most importantly, for our purposes, any footpath or bridleway which was in existence on 31 December 1959. (Please see below under "Responsibility for footpaths and bridleways".)

Therefore the only footpaths and bridleways which are not maintainable at the public expense are those paths or ways which have come into existence since 1959 and have not been constructed, adopted or maintained by a highway authority, or created under a public path creation agreement or order or under a section 38 agreement.

Long distance routes

Sections 50A–55 of the National Parks and Access to the Countryside Act 1949 made provision for the implementation of long distance routes. Such implementation was to be instigated by the Countryside Commission "where it appears to the commission ... that the public should be enabled to make extensive journeys on foot or on horseback [or on a bicycle] ..."

The machinery for the provision of the long distance routes is that the Countryside Commission, after approval by the Secretary of State, seeks the implementation of the route by local highway authorities. The local highway authorities have to use the normal means at their disposal, such as public path creation, and diversion orders, or creation by agreement.[1] There is no special power of implementation. The Countryside Commission can provide funding.

[1] As to which see Chap 3.

Maintenance
Maintenance includes repair and the terms "maintain" and "maintainable" are to be construed accordingly.

Public path
Is defined in the Wildlife and Countryside Act 1981 as a highway being either a footpath or a bridleway.

Public right of way
A way over which the public have the right to pass and repass. As a matter of convention this term is normally reserved for footpaths and bridleways, (and sometimes roads used as public paths).

Road
There is no definition of "road" in the Highways Act.

There is a definition of "road" which occurs in the Road Traffic Regulation Act 1984 and the Road Traffic Act 1988 which says that "road" means any highway and any other road to which the public has access and includes bridges over which a road passes."[2] Under statutory interpretation a footpath or bridleway is both a road and a street, which does not accord with ordinary usage.

Road used as a public path
This is not defined in the Highways Act 1980 (or in the Wildlife and Countryside Act 1981 in any helpful way) but is in fact a road (as to which see above) which is used mainly by either pedestrians or pedestrians and equestrians but over which vehicular rights may exist. By the Wildlife and Countryside Act 1981 it should be shown in the definitive plan as a byway open to all traffic or a bridleway or footpath.[3] Such roads are known as Rupps.

Street
In the Highways Act 1980 it is stated that this term has the same meaning as in Part III of the New Roads and Street Works Act 1991.

Section 48(1) in Part III of the New Roads and Street Works Act 1991 states as follows:

[2] s 142
[3] s 54(2) and (3)

"... A street means the whole or any part of any of the following, irrespective of whether it is a thoroughfare–
> (a) any highway, road, lane, footway, alleyway or passage
> (b) any square or court, and
> (c) any land laid out as a way whether it is for the time being formed as a way or not.

Where a street passes over a bridge or through a tunnel, references in this part to the street include that bridge or tunnel".

As with "road", this has the curious result that a footpath and bridleway is a street whereas the everyday use of the word is closer to "Town or village road that has (mainly) contiguous houses on one side or both" (*Concise Oxford Dictionary*).

Traffic
"Includes pedestrians and animals"

Walkway
Walkways are frequently to be found in shopping precincts. Walkways are unusual in that whilst they have some of the features of footpaths, they are situated inside buildings. Section 35 of the Highways Act 1980 enables a person having an interest in land to enter into an agreement with a highway authority (or a district council after consultation with the highway authority) for the provision of a way over through or under parts of buildings etc. It also provides for the dedication by that person of those ways as footpaths "subject to such limitations and conditions as ... may be specified ...". Typically, provision is made for the closure of the walkways when the shops are not open.

The Nature of Footpaths and Bridleways

As is clear from the definitions given above from the Highways Act, footpath and bridleways are highways. They are ways over which the public has a right of way to pass and repass. If the use of the way is limited to a certain group of people then it is not a highway. (Of course, private paths may be called footpaths or bridleways and that is perfectly acceptable use of the words. But for the purposes of this book "footpath" and "bridleway" have the same meanings as are found in the Highways Act.) Moreover that right is not limited in time. The adage "once a highway always a highway" comes from the common law and is still valid. Normally the only way in which a highway can cease to be a highway is by a closure procedure laid down by statute and involving an order of a highway authority or of a court. It is true that highways can cease to be highways be disappearing, *e.g.* by falling into the sea, but not by falling into disuse.

Frequently footpaths and bridleways are "invisible" in that they are not marked out on the ground so that there is nothing to distinguish them from surrounding land. It is therefore often very difficult to see exactly where the path or way runs, let alone what width it is. Where a path or way runs over grass there is nothing illegal about this, but where a path or way runs over cultivated land and the farmer exercises the right to plough the land under section 134 of the Highways Act 1980 he is obliged to make good the surface of the path and to indicate the line of the path or way on the ground to not less than its minimum width.

A footpath and bridleway may be any width consistent with being a "way" or route. That is, it cannot be simply an area of land over which there is a right to wander. Frequently the width of a footpath and bridleway will be hard to gauge from looking at it. In some cases the width will appear obvious because there are what appear to be boundaries, such as fences or hedges on both sides. In such cases there is a presumption that the footpath and bridleway is bounded by the fences.

In Schedule 12 of the Highways Act there are provisions as to maximum and minimum widths where works of reinstatement of highways are to be carried out. These provisions only in effect apply to highways where there is no proved width. The maximum and minimum widths are as follows:

- field edge footpaths: minimum 1.5 metres, maximum 1.8 metres;
- field edge bridleways: minimum 3 metres maximum 3 metres;
- other footpaths: minimum 1 metre, maximum 1.8 metres;
- other bridleways: minimum 2 metres maximum 3 metres.

Responsibility for Footpaths and Bridleways

The *National Parks and Access to the Countryside Act 1949* made all footpaths and bridleways in existence at that time (or coming into existence thereafter by way of certain statutory procedures) publicly maintainable. The *Highways Act 1959* repealed the provision, but all footpaths and bridleways in existence on 31 December 1959 remained publicly maintainable and remain so by virtue of section 38 of the Highways Act. As noted above, the upshot of this is that the vast majority of footpaths and bridleways remain publicly maintainable. Where a footpath and bridleway has been created by dedication and agreement since 31 December 1959, it will not *prima facie* be publicly maintainable.[4] However the highway authority has various powers under the Highways Act to adopt footpaths and bridleways.

Prior to the passing of the Highways Act 1959, where a highway was publicly maintainable it was to be maintained by the inhabitants at large. The Highways Act of 1959 – which has been largely reenacted within the Highways Act 1980 – replaced the concept of "repairable by the inhabitants at large" with "maintainable at the public expense", and it imposed on the highway authority the duty of maintaining such highways.

The Highway Authority therefore has the responsibility for maintaining the vast majority of footpath and bridleways and ensuring that they are kept in good repair and remain unobstructed.[5] District Councils have the power to maintain footpath and bridleways in their areas[6], and to be reimbursed for so doing by their highway authorities[7]; and parish councils have also the right to maintain footpath and bridleways in their areas[8], but do not have the right to be reimbursed (although they may be reimbursed).

The Three Interests

It will be appreciated from the above that there are three main legal interests in highways.

1. The public which use the highway as of right to pass and repass. The public have certain responsibilities for their behaviour on the highway as well as limitations on their rights.
2. The owner of the land over which the highway passes. Again, the owner has responsibilities towards the public. In relation to some highways, now a very small minority, the owner of land has also the responsibility of maintenance and repair. In the case of rural footpath and bridleways the owner of land is clearly likely to be closely concerned with the use and condition of the highway which runs over his land. In urban areas where frontagers may only own

---

[4]See Chap 3
[5]Highways Act 1980 s 130
[6]Highways Act 1980 ss 42 and 50
[7]Highways Act 1980 Sched 7
[8]Highways Act 1980 s 43

a small part of the subsoil under the highway, the involvement with the highway may appear to be nothing more or less than proximity.

3. The highway authority. The highway authority is a hybrid. In some sense it is a development from the inhabitants at large, who were obliged to maintain highways once they had been dedicated to them by the landowner. The very phrase "inhabitants at large" suggests its closeness to the public which uses the highway. In another sense the highway authority is closer in concept to the landowner and indeed is the owner of the surface of the highway under section 263 of the Highways Act. The highway authority is sometimes also the owner of the subsoil, particularly of new roads, although far less frequently of footpath and bridleways.

This tripartite relationship, and its development from what was essentially a relationship between landowner and public has to be kept in mind when trying to understand what sometimes appear to be the somewhat haphazard set of laws relating to the maintenance and use of highways.

It should perhaps be mentioned there is a fourth special interest in many highways namely that of statutory undertakers. However the interest of statutory undertakers has comparatively little consequence for the development of highway law or its understanding, and even less for the law of footpaths and bridleways and will not be dealt with here.

Footpaths and bridleways coming into existence since 31 December 1959 will be publicly maintainable if they are constructed by a Highways Authority, or if they result from a Creation Order or Diversion Order under Highways Act 1980 or the Town and Country Planning Act 1990 or a public path creation agreement under section 25 of the Highways Act (and under some other statutory provisions).

Landowner, Public and Highway Authority

CHAPTER 2

Landowner, Public and Highway Authority

The curious tripartite relationship between landowner public and highway authority has been mentioned in the first chapter. We will now look in turn at the roles and responsibilities of the three participants.

The Landowner

Where a footpath or bridleway is maintainable at the public expense the surface of the highway is owned by the highway authority. The subsoil is normally owned (and is presumed to be owned) by the owner of the land through which the highway passes. Where there are different owners of the land on either side of the highway there is a presumption that each adjacent owner owns the land up to the middle line.[1] It could be argued that this presumption would be rebutted by showing that a previous owner of the land including the land under the highway conveyed only the land on one side of the road thus retaining the ownership of the strip under the highway. Where a highway has been laid out by a developer it is often the case that the developer has retained ownership of the subsoil of the highway.

Ownership of the subsoil may appear to be of somewhat academic interest. However there are situations in which it becomes important. Where a highway is extinguished, the surface of the highway reverts to the ownership of the owner of the subsoil. This reversion occurs automatically, without need for conveyance.

Another feature of ownership of the subsoil is that it appears to be capable of sustaining an action for trespass against those who abuse their right to pass and repass along the highway.[2] This may appear somewhat

---

[1] *St Edmundsbury Board of Finance v Clark* [1973] 1 WLR 1572
[2] See *e.g. Hickman* v *Maisey* [1900] 1 QB 752 and the discussion in Chap 8.

curious since the trespass appears to be to the surface and not to the subsoil. Please see the discussion of *Hickman* v *Maisey* below.

Access to the highway

Ownership of the land adjacent to the highway carries with it the right to have access to the highway. However this right has in effect been curtailed by the consideration that the formation of a new access to the highway is a development for the purposes of planning law and thus may require planning permission.

Burdens of ownership

Burdens also attach to ownership of land adjoining the highway. The landowner must maintain his land so that it does not cause a nuisance to users of the highway.

In particular he must:

- maintain his land in a reasonably safe condition so that no injury is caused to users of the highway[3];
- maintain trees on his land so that they do not cause injury to passers by[4] or damage to the highway by their roots or falling branches[5];
- prevent water from his land from being discharged onto the highway when a notice is served on him by a local authority[6];
- remove barbed wire on his land if it causes a nuisance to the highway and he is required to remove it by a local authority.[7]

The right to plough

In certain circumstances agricultural landowners will have the right to plough and otherwise disturb the surface of footpaths and bridleways over their land. This right is subject to the duty to reinstate the footpath and bridleway after it has been disturbed. This is discussed in Chapter 6.

The Public

Members of the public have the right to pass and repass along the highway. According to whether the way is a footpath or bridleway, the members of

---

[3]At common law and under Highways Act 1980 s 165 when required by notice from the local authority.
[4]*Caminer* v *Northern & London Investment Trust Ltd* [1951] AC 88
[5]*Butler* v *Standard Telephones and Cables* [1940] 1 KB 399
[6]Highways Act 1980 s 163
[7]Highways Act 1980 s 164

the public will have the right only to walk; or to walk and ride on horseback or on a bicycle.

At common law the greater rights have always included the lesser, so that whereas the right to pass on foot did not necessarily indicate the existence of other rights, the right to ride on horseback always included the right to go on foot.

Not all manner of passing and repassing is permitted.

Trespass
If a member of the public abuses the right to pass and repass, then he will be a trespasser.

Harrison v Duke of Rutland [1893] 1 QB 142
The plaintiff lingered on a highway which passed over the defendant's grouse moor for the sole and express purpose of interfering with the defendant's right of shooting over the moor. The plaintiff was turned off the land by the defendant's gamekeepers and the plaintiff sued the defendant for assault. The defendant counter-claimed in trespass.

It was held that the plaintiff was a trespasser since he was using the highway to do acts other than were reasonable and usual and interfering with the defendant's rightful enjoyment of his land.

Hickman v Maisey [1900] 1 QB 752
The plaintiff owned land which was crossed by a highway. A racehorse trainer used some of the land for the training and trial of racehorses. A view of that land could be had from the highway. The defendant was one of the proprietors of a racing journal. On the occasion in question the defendant walked up and down a 15 yard stretch of the highway for about an hour and a half watching and taking note of the racehorse trials.

When the plaintiff sued him for trespass it was held that the defendant had exceeded the ordinary and reasonable user of a highway as such to which the public are entitled and he was therefore guilty of a trespass on the plaintiff's land. It was said that this case was very close to *Harrison v Duke of Rutland*.

Hubbard v Pitt [1975] 2 WLR 254
The defendants were pickets from a group of people disapproving of the activities of estate agents who assisted property developers in their area. The defendants picketed the estate agents by standing outside their offices in a line on the footway, holding placards and distributing leaflets. They left

room for pedestrians to walk along the footway. The estate agents brought the action for an injunction. The were granted the interlocutory injunction.

It was held that the common law right was the right to use a highway for passing and repassing. Any other user not ordinarily and reasonably incidental to that right was a trespass and unlawful unless authorised by statute. (It was also held that the picketing amounted to a public nuisance.)

It is something of a curiosity that these cases make it clear that the trespass by a member of the public who abuses the right to pass and repass is against the owner of subsoil, *i.e.* the owner of the land surrounding or on one side of the footpath and bridleway (it will be remembered that in the latter case the adjacent owner owns the path or way up to the middle line). Since the trespass appears to be to the topsoil of the highway and not to the subsoil it would appear more logical if the trespass were held to be against the highway authority.

Taking rest on the highway
Whilst members of the public have the right to pass and repass it is not clear that they have the right to take any rest on the highway. However in *Hickman* v *Maisey*, it was said that "if a man, while using the highway for passage, sat down for a time to rest himself, to call that trespass would be unreasonable" (*per* Lord Justice Smith at p 756). It would therefore appear that to take rest on the highway is permissible if it is ancillary to passage along the highway. However if that is the criterion, it would appear to allow a pedestrian on a long journey to sleep overnight on the highway – which may not be what Lord Justice Smith intended.

Whilst users of the highway have the right to use the highway and to have it maintained to the appropriate standard, it is also a well-established principle that the public must take a highway as it finds it. Therefore it would appear that where a landowner dedicates a highway across his land subject to the highway being impassable in the winter, that is how the public must accept it if it chooses to accept it at all.

Usual accompaniments
Users of highways do have the right to take with them the "usual accompaniments" such as dogs. But the dog must remain on the line of the path. Such a dog need not generally be on a lead, but the highway authority does have the power under section 27 of the Road Traffic Act 1988 to make an order requiring dogs to be kept on leads on specified rights of way.

Section 1(2)(c) of the Dogs (Protection of Livestock) Act 1953 makes it an offence to allow a dog to be at large on a field or enclosure where there are sheep. There are exception to this general rule for police dogs, trained sheep dogs etc.

In *R* v *Matthias* (1861) 2 F&F 570, NP a jury found that the small perambulator was an "usual accompaniment", if of a size and weight not to inconvenience other passengers, and not to injure the soil.

Bulls
The public are entitled to use footpaths and bridleways free from fear of bulls. It is an offence under the Wildlife and Countryside Act 1981 for the occupier of a field which is crossed by a right of way to keep a bull in the field. There are exceptions, which include bulls under 10 months old.

Motor vehicles
Driving a motor vehicle on a footpath and bridleway "without lawful authority" is an offence under section 34 of the Road Traffic Act 1988.

Bicycles
It has been seen that bicycles are allowed on bridleways but must give way to equestrians. It is an offence under the Road Traffic Act 1988 to ride a bicycle on a bridleway recklessly (s 28), or without due care and attention or without reasonable consideration for other road users (s 29) or whilst unfit to ride through drink or drugs (s 30).

However the riding of a bicycle is not permitted on a footpath and the rider of a bicycle on a footpath would commit trespass against the owner of the land over which the footpath runs. It is unlikely that a pedal cycle constitutes an "usual accompaniment" so as to allow it to be pushed on a footpath.

Horses on footpaths
Riding or leading a horse on a footpath constitutes a trespass against the owner(s) of the land on which the footpath is situated.

Abatement of nuisances
A member of the public who comes across an obstruction of a footpath and bridleway is entitled to remove it since under common law an obstruction of the highway or any thing which renders the highway dangerous is a nuisance and attracts the right of users of the highway to abate it.

James v Hayward 1630 Cro Car 184
It was held that if a new gate is erected across a public highway it constitutes a public nuisance even though it be not fastened, and any of the King's subjects passing that way may cut it down and destroy it.

However it appears that an obstruction which occurs as the result of mere non-feasance may not be abated by constructive work.

Campbell Davys v Lloyd [1901] 2 Ch 518
The plaintiff and the defendant were neighbours, their property being separated by a river over which there had passed a footbridge which carried a footpath. The defendant reinstated the footbridge, cutting into the plaintiff's land and constructed thereon a platform for the bridge. The plaintiff sued.

It was held that a person who is merely entitled as one of the public to use a bridge carrying the highway over a river is not justified in entering on another person's land, and re-erecting a bridge which has been allowed to fall into a state of decay. An operation of this nature cannot properly fall under the term "abatement" even if the right to "abate" exists at all, in the case of a nuisance arising from mere non-feasance.

Section 333 of the Highways Act preserves the right of abatement, stating that:

> "No provision of this Act relating to obstruction of or other interference with highways is to be taken to affect any right of a highway authority or other person under any enactment not contained in this Act, or under any other rule of law, to remove an obstruction from the highway or otherwise abate a nuisance ..."

Anyone who abates a nuisance in this way clearly runs the risk that in doing so they may be committing a trespass, if they cannot subsequently justify their action. The more cautious, whether public authority or individual, might prefer to seek a judicial decision as counselled by Lord Russell CJ in *Reynolds* v *Presteign Urban District Council* [1896] 1 QB 604.

Negotiating obstructions
Apart from the right of abatement, does a user of the footpath and bridleway have the right to go off the path or way when he cannot go on along the line of the path or way on account of an obstruction?

Arnold v Holbrook (1873) LR 8 QB 96
There was a public footpath across the field of the appellant, but subject to his right to plough. The appellant ploughed the field but did not reinstate it, leaving the public to walk it in. As a result, the footpath became very muddy and users started to deviate and walk on either side. The appellant placed hurdles on either side of the path to prevent the deviation and when the respondent threw down the hurdles the appellant sued.

The appellate court found that the appellant had the right to place the hurdles.

However, it appears from *Stacey* v *Sherrin* (1913) 29 TLR 555 that if the obstruction is put there by the landowner the public have the right to deviate around it. But if the obstruction occurs through natural causes, there may be no right to deviate (*Taylor* v *Whitehead* [1781] 2 Doug KB 745).

The Highway Authority

The highway authority has wide and onerous responsibilities and extensive powers in relation to footpaths and bridleways. These are supplemented by some functions which are given to local councils, *e.g,* district councils. The responsibilities and powers of the highway authority may be summarised as follows.

Responsibilities

- To assert and protect the rights of passage

  Under section 130 of the Highways Act 1980 it is the duty of the highway authority to assert and protect the rights of the public to the use and enjoyment of any highway for which they are the highway authority.

  Under subsection (3) of the section, a highway authority also has the duty to prevent as far as possible the stopping up or obstruction of highways in their area.

  There are many provisions under the Highways Act 1980 and other legislation dealing with obstructions of the highway. Section 137 of the Highways Act makes it a specific offence to "wilfully obstruct free passage along a highway". The use of force or threats against users of the highway may additionally constitute the tort of trespass or an offence under the Public Order Act 1986. It is also a public nuisance to obstruct the highway. Nuisances are dealt with in Chapter 6.

- To maintain footpaths and bridleways

  This is a very wide-ranging and onerous responsibility which it dealt with at length in Chapter 5.

- To record footpaths and bridleways

  The highway authority has the duty, imposed by section 36(6) of the Highways Act, to keep a list of all highways maintainable at the public expense. They also have the duty, as surveying authority, to keep the definitive map of footpaths and bridleways and continuously review it. Details are to be found in Chapter 4.

- To signpost and waymark footpaths and bridleways

  Section 68 of the Countryside Act 1968 requires highway authorities to mark footpaths and bridleways. Details of this requirement are also to be found in Chapter 4.

Powers

The powers given to highway authorities are often connected with their duties although the often go beyond their express duties in scope.

- Improvement

  This power is closely associated with the duties and powers of maintenance and is set out in Chapter 5.

- Creation, diversion and extinguishment

  These powers are given to highway and in some cases other authorities under provisions of the Highways Act and other legislation. They normally involve the making of Orders followed by a well-defined statutory procedure which allows for objection and may lead to a local public inquiry. These subjects are dealt with in Chapters 3, 7, and 9.

- Legal action

  Closely associated with their obligation to assert and protect the rights of the public, highway authorities are giving the power to prosecute for a large number of offences, and they may take civil action in the courts to obtain injunctions, damages etc.

- Direct action to remove obstructions

  In clear cases of obstruction of a highway, the highway authority may remove the obstruction without recourse to legal proceedings (see *Reynolds* v *Presteign, supra*).

Incidents of ownership

As well as having statutory duties and powers, a highway authority is the owner of the topsoil of highways maintainable at the public expense (s 263(1) of the Highways Act). However a highway authority is somewhat limited in its enjoyment of ownership. It can only use the highway land as highway and can only act within its statutory powers otherwise its acts will be *ultra vires* and may well constitute an interference with the rights of the public.

Trespass

It was doubtful whether a highway authority could maintain an action in trespass (contrast with the position of the owner of the land described above[8]). However this has been resolved by:

Wiltshire CC v Frazer (1984) P & CR 69

Caravan dwellers pitched their caravans and tents within the limits of the highway. The County Council started proceedings for summary possession under order 113 of the Rules of the Supreme Court.

The Court of Appeal held that the County Council's fee simple gave them a sufficient interest to maintain an action in trespass and therefore to succeed in the application.

In some cases the highway authority will own the subsoil as well as the topsoil, for example where the highway authority has constructed a road and has acquired the land by compulsory purchase.

[8]*Hickman v Maisey, supra*

How Footpaths and Bridleways are Created

How Footpaths and Bridleways are Created

For many centuries highways were created predominantly as the result of dedication and acceptance. That is to say they came into being as the result of what was in effect an agreement between the landowner and the public who wished to use his land for passage. Nowadays a way or path is much more likely to be created as the result of the more formal process of a creation order or agreement, as the result of the building of a new carriageway (probably after the making of Compulsory Purchase Orders and Side Roads Orders) or after the laying out of a new estate (these last two processes do in fact involve a more formalised version of dedication and acceptance).

Dedication and Acceptance

This involves a dedication or giving by the owner of the land and acceptance by the public. Dedication simply means the granting by the owner of the right to use the way over his land. Acceptance means that the offer is taken up by the public in that they use the way that has been dedicated.

In order for dedication and acceptance to take place, the freehold owner of land must dedicate the land as a public right of way, that is, it must be for the public at large (and not just for persons of a particular group or class such as the inhabitants of a parish or hamlet), and it must be for all time, not just for, say, 100 years. The dedication may, however, be subject to limitation or condition. Thus, the right of way that is created may be subject to existing use. To take what used to be a quite common example, the public using a tow-path may have had to give precedence to barge operators driving their horses to pull barges. Also the dedication may be for only the classes of traffic (as opposed to the classes of persons) which the owner chooses, such as pedestrians, pedestrians and equestrians etc.

Express dedication

There are no formalities required for an express dedication, which is likely to be a written statement by the owner indicating that the way shown on the attached plan is dedicated as a footpath or bridleway.

Presumed dedication

Common law

More frequently, paths or ways will have to be shown to have been dedicated by inference or presumption. As a matter of common law the proof that a way has been used as of right by the public has served as proof that there was an intention to dedicate. This presumption does not require any particular period of use, but the use must be of sufficient length to raise the inference that the freehold owner intended to dedicate the way as a highway. The presumption is rebuttable. In *Greenwich Board of Works* v *Maudslay* (1870) LR 5 QB 397, Lord Blackburn said:

> "It is necessary to show, in order that there may be a right of way established, that it has been used openly as of right and for so long a time that it must have come to the knowledge of the owners of the fee that the public were so using it as of right, and from this apparent acquiescence of the owners a jury might fairly draw the inference that they chose to consent, in which case there would be a dedication."

Rebuttal will take the form of showing that there was no intention to dedicate to the public at large. This may be done by showing that the owner of the land has turned back users of the path or way; or by showing that he has erected obstructions to prevent it being used as a public path or way. It may also be shown that the apparent dedicator did not have the capacity to dedicate, as where land is held in strict settlement or is owned by a public body whose purposes are incompatible with dedication to the public at large (*BTC* v *Westmoreland County Council* [1958] AC 126). The owner may also show that he has restricted the use of the way to a class of persons such as the inhabitants of a village, so that it has not been dedicated to the public at large.

By statute: sections 31 and 32 of the Highways Act 1980

Section 31 of the Highways Act puts the presumption of dedication on a statutory footing, with slight differences. The section provides that where a way over any land has been actually enjoyed by the public as of right and without interruption for a full period of 20 years the way is to be deemed to have been dedicated as a highway unless there is sufficient evidence that there was no intention during that period to dedicate it. This does not apply to any situation where a presumption of dedication could not arise at common law (such as where the person who appears to have dedicated it had no power to dedicate). This statutory provision is an alternative and an addition to the common law rules governing the ways in which a right of way may be proved.

Subsection (3) of section 31 states that the presumption that a way is a highway may be negatived by the owner of the land over which the claimed highway passes erecting and maintaining a suitable notice to show that he does not intend to dedicate the way as a highway. An owner of land is also enabled by subsection (6) to deposit with the appropriate council a map of his land together with a declaration that he has no intention to dedicate ways over his land other than any highways which may already be in existence.

The application of section 31 was considered in the case of *Fairey* v *Southampton County Council* [1956] 2 QB 439. In that case it was held that the 20 year period is to be reckoned backwards from the date on which the existence of the path or way was brought into question. It was also made clear that for a landowner to turn back the odd user of the highway such as a stranger to the locality would not be enough. The landowner must make it clear to the public that there was no right of way. In certain situations that would involve making it known to local users. The case also indicated that there must be some overt acts on the part of the landowner to negative the intention to dedicate. It was not enough that in his own mind he did not intend to dedicate.

However where the landowner does commit acts which clearly imply that he has no intention to dedicate, they will suffice even if they are short-lived. For example the closing of a way on one day a year will suffice (*Chinnock* v *Hartley-Wintney RDC* (1899) 63 JP 327).

Acceptance

Dedication on its own is not sufficient to create a highway. In order to become a highway the way must be accepted by the public. The traditional method of acceptance by the public has been simply use by the public of the highway as of right. There is clearly a close relationship between dedication and acceptance in so far as dedication is often proved by evidence of use which is also evidence of acceptance.

Proving Dedication

Disputes as to whether a footpath and bridleway exists have been reduced by the advent of definitive maps. Where a highway is shown on a definitive map, that serves as conclusive proof that the highway exists as shown until such time as the Map and Statement are changed. However the absence of a footpath and bridleway on the definitive map and statement do not prove that a route does not exist; and there still occur disputes as to whether a path or way exists, whether for the purposes of a modification order or otherwise.

User evidence
Normally the substance of evidence relied upon to prove the existence of a right of way will be the evidence of users of the path or way. This may be supplemented where appropriate by photographs and records including letters, memos and so on. Hearsay evidence may normally be relied upon depending upon the forum in which the claim is heard, although in principle, and often in practice, this is likely to carry less weight than oral evidence. However, in certain circumstances hearsay evidence, particularly contemporary records, may be very telling.

Location of the path or way
Where a path or way leads may be of relevance. As a general rule, where a path or way leads to a main road it is more likely that it is a highway than if it leads to a church or a couple of houses.

R v Enfield Inhabitants (1819)
This case was cited in Burn's *Justice of the Peace*, 30th ed at p 991n. Where a way leads to a market town or communicates with a great road, it is a highway, but if it leads to a church, to a particular house, to a village or to a field, it is a private way. But it is a matter of fact and much depends upon common reputation.

Capacity of the landowner
Where the land over which the footpath and bridleway is claimed to run has been in strict settlement, that will be of relevance (although probably not decisive) as to whether it is a highway. The case of *Williams-Ellis* v *Cobb* is germane both to this issue and to the previous issue as to where a way leads.

Williams-Ellis v Cobb [1935] 1 KB 310
The plaintiff claimed damages against several defendants for trespassing over his land and sought an injunction. The defendants contended that they were using a public right of way. Evidence was given of public user by five different classes of persons over the whole period of living memory, of two defined ways over the plaintiff's land from a public high road to the sea at high-water mark. It was also proved that the plaintiff's land was in strict settlement from 1856 to 1908 and that during that period there was never an owner capable of dedication.

It was held on appeal that:

1. The sea was a sufficient *terminus ad quem* for a public way even though it does not lead to a public place; and that
2. Where there is evidence of public user of a way throughout the period of living memory, but there being no owner capable of dedication during that period the court may infer a dedication by an owner capable of dedication at some date anterior to the earliest proved user; but that
3. There is no presumption to compel the court to draw such an inference even from unrebutted evidence of long-continued and uninterrupted user.

Maps, plans and histories as evidence
Section 32 of the Highways Act makes provision for the reception of maps, plans and histories of the locality by any court or tribunal determining whether a way has been dedicated as a highway. This is an important evidential provision since maps, plans and histories are very often hearsay and may well involve double hearsay. It is frequently the case that the court or tribunal which is asked to receive maps plans and histories has very little information as to their provenance or status, and would be in considerable difficulty as to their admission in the absence of this section.

Creation of Highways by Statute

Public path creation agreements
Section 25 of the Highways Act allows for a local authority (*i.e.* County Council, District Council, London Borough Council etc) to enter into an agreement with any person having the necessary power in that behalf (normally the owner of the land in fee simple) for the dedication by that person of a footpath or bridleway in their area. This is called a public path creation agreement. Such an agreement may be subject to limitations or conditions and to payment. As with dedication and acceptance the limitations

and conditions must not relate to classes of users (as opposed to mode of use such as horseback, bicycle etc) but may concern such matters as the giving of precedence to existing users, giving way to waterway traffic when a swing bridge is in use and so on.

Section 30 of the Highways Act allows parish and community councils to enter into agreements for the dedication of a highway in the same way that local authorities may under section 25.

Public path creation orders

Section 26 of the Highways Act gives powers to a local authority to create a footpath or bridleway where it appears that there is a need for one and it is expedient to create one, having regard for the convenience and enjoyment of persons living in the area etc and having regard to the effect on the rights of persons interested in the land over which the right of way would pass. The right of way is created by order which has to be submitted to the Secretary of State for approval. Schedule 6 to the Act lays down the procedure for publication and confirmation of orders and the consideration of representations and objections.

Diversions of existing footpaths and bridleways

A diversion of a highway can be broken down into two parts, namely the stopping up of an existing highway or a part of it, and the provision of a new stretch of highway by way of substitution for the old.

Part VIII of the Highways Act 1980 deals with stopping up and diversions of highways. The principal sections which deal with the diversion of footpaths and bridleways are:

- section 116, supplemented by section 117, which allows a magistrates' court to stop up or divert a highway;
- section 119 which allows for the diversion of footpaths and bridleways;
- section 119A which allows for the diversion of footpaths and bridleways which cross railways other than by tunnels or bridges.

Section 116
Section 116 of the Act provides that

> "... if it appears to a Magistrates' Court, after a view, if the Court thinks fit, by any two or more of the justices composing the Court, that a highway ...
>> (b) can be diverted so as to make it nearer or more commodious to the public, the Court may by Order authorise it to be ... so diverted."

The procedure under this section can only be initiated by the highway authority.

Notices
Provision is made for the giving of notices to the relevant district and parish councils, which have a right of veto.

Notice has to be given to owners and occupiers of adjoining lands, to statutory undertakers with apparatus under the highway, in the *London Gazette*, and in at least one local newspaper. Notice also has to be displayed in a prominent position at the ends of the highway.

Hearing
On the hearing of the application all the persons who have a right to be served with the notices, together with any person who uses the highway and any other person who would be aggrieved by the Order have a right to be heard. If the magistrates make the Order these people have a right of appeal to the Crown Court against the making of the Order (whether or not they have appeared before the magistrates).

Where an Order for a diversion is made, the written consent of every landowner over whose land the diversion (*i.e.* new path or way) is to lie must be obtained.

In making a diversion Order, the magistrates can reserve a right of way as footpath or bridleway so that the stopping up or diversion is limited in effect. This means that they can, for example, divert a bridleway but leave intact pedestrian rights, or divert a carriageway but leave intact bridleway rights.

Although the application under section 116 is limited to highway authorities, another person may request the highway authority to make such an application and if it does so, the highway authority may require that person to make provision for the costs of the application.

There are other powers of diversion in section 247 of the Town and Country Planning Act 1990 (as to which see Chap 7).

There is also the power in section 257 of the Town and Country Planning Act 1990 for the creation of an alternative highway for use as a replacement of a highway which is being stopped up or diverted under the same section.

Sections 119 and 119A
Sections 119 and 119A of the Highways Act provide a different kind of procedure, namely a diversion of a footpath or bridleway by Order of a Council. (In this context "Council" includes County and District Councils.) Such an Order can only be made where it appears to a Council that in the interests of the owner, lessee or occupier of land crossed by the path or way or of the public, it is expedient that the line of the path or way, or part of that line could be diverted (whether on to land of the same or another owner, lessee or occupier). It needs to be confirmed by the council itself if unopposed, or by the Secretary of State if opposed. Before confirming the Order, the Council or Secretary of State must be satisfied that:

1. It is expedient as set out above that the path or way be diverted; and
2. The path or way will not be substantially less convenient to the public in consequence of the diversion and that it is expedient to confirm the order having regard to the effect which:
   (a) the effect which the diversion would have on the enjoyment of the path or way as a whole;
   (b) the coming into operation of the order would have as respects other land served by the existing public right of way, and
   (c) any new public right of way created by the order would have as respects the land over which the right is so created and any land held with it;
   but for the purposes of (b) and (c) the provisions of the section as regards compensation may be taken into account.

Further information concerning the procedure for making such orders is given in Chapter 7.

Construction by highway authorities
Construction of highways may be undertaken by local councils and housing action trusts under Housing Act powers where the construction is carried out to the satisfaction of the highway authority.

Section 38 agreements
Section 38 of the Highways Act provides for an agreement between the highway authority and a person who proposes to dedicate or construct and then dedicate. This section is of considerable practical value and is normally used when a developer proposes to construct a highway for subsequent

adoption by the highway authority. Such agreements frequently provide for a charge to by made by the highway authority to the developer. No doubt this section is used far more often for roads with carriageways than for footpath and bridleways.

Side roads Orders

Sections 14 and 18 of the Highways Act confer important powers on highway authorities in relation to trunk and classified roads. Highway authorities are empowered to stop up, divert, improve, raise, lower or otherwise alter a highway that enters or crosses the route of trunk roads and classified roads and to construct new highways for the purposes of diverting, improving etc such (subsidiary) roads. Such measures are achieved by the making of Orders and the procedure for the making of the Orders is provided by Schedule 1 of the Act. These powers are frequently used for the creation of footpaths and bridleways as well as for carriageways. If any appreciable length of new road is planned it is very likely that it will cross the route of footpaths and/or bridleways. The highway authority, whether it is the Minister (in the case of trunk roads) or the local highway authority in the case of other classified roads, will have to make provision for alternative routes to the footpaths and bridleways which are having to be stopped up to accommodate the new road.

Section 14(6) and section 18(6) provide that no Order under these sections authorising the stopping up of a highway shall be made or confirmed by the Minister unless he is satisfied that another reasonably convenient route is available or will be provided before the highway is stopped up. Sometimes a reasonably convenient alternative already exists, but frequently an alternative will have to be provided.

Diversion along new highway

Very often the route which is provided by the highway authority consists of a diversion along the new road to a roundabout or other convenient crossing point and then back along the other side of the new road to the location where the footpath and bridleway had originally been departed from. Whether such a diversion (often along a busy new road where the original footpath and bridleway had consisted of a country ramble) will provide a "reasonably convenient" alternative tends to form a lively basis for dispute at public inquiries. Obviously a good deal depends on the length of the diversion. It should be noted that what is required is an alternative route, not an alternative path or way which is of the same status as the route which is being replaced. Usually the type of provision which has just been described involves the replacement of a footpath with a length of footway which is within the boundaries of the proposed new road.

Similarly, equestrians who previously had to share their bridleways only with pedestrians and cyclists may find themselves having to ride for some distance along the new carriageway (where it is a dual carriageway) and back again. However, section 71 places a duty on the highway authority to provide in or by the side of a highway which comprises a made up carriageway adequate grass or other margin as part of the highway where they consider the provision of margins necessary or desirable for the safety or accommodation of ridden horses. This section does not cater expressly for dual carriageways but may be of particular relevance to such roads, where speeds of motorists are likely to be higher, and perhaps the expectation of encountering equestrians lower. Even where such a margin is provided it may be removed by the highway authority at a later date, so that again the equestrians obtaining such provision are arguably getting something which is considerably less desirable than that which was provided by the bridleway.

Town and Country Planning Act
Section 248 of the Town and Country Planning Act 1990 contains similar measures to sections 14 and 18 for the making of Side Roads Orders where planning permission has been granted for the construction or improvement of a highway.

Section 257 of the Town and Country Planning Act allows for diversion (as well as stopping up) of footpaths and bridleways if it is necessary to enable development to be carried out. This section provides a variation from other sections permitting stopping up and diversion in that it additionally allows for the creation of alternative highways as replacements for the ones to be stopped up or diverted. This differs from a diversion in that where a way is diverted, only part of the path or way is replaced.

Other powers
There are various other powers which enable highways to be created including the Civil Aviation Act 1982, the Water Act 1989 section 155 and section 211 of the Church Property (Miscellaneous Provisions) Measure 1960. Public Rights of Way may also be created by Acts of Parliament.

Compensation
Compensation is also payable in relation to public path creation orders made under section 26 where the claimant can show that there is a

depreciation in the value of his interest in land or that he has suffered damage by being disturbed in his enjoyment of land as a result of the order.

Compensation is payable where land is compulsorily purchased.

No compensation is payable under section 30 (dedication by agreement with parish and community councils), or under sections 247 and 248 (in relation to diversions) of the Town and Country Planning Act 1990.

Mapping and Marking

CHAPTER 4

Mapping and Marking

Mapping of Footpaths and Bridleways

Definitive maps

Under the *National Parks and Access to the Countryside Act 1949* the County Councils as surveying authorities were required to survey and record on a map all those footpaths, bridleways and Rupps which, in the opinion of the County Councils, were reasonably alleged to be public rights of way. It took a very long time for all the County Councils to comply with this requirement, but the great majority of *rural* areas had been surveyed by 1982.

The procedure under the National Parks and Access to the Countryside Act 1949 was somewhat elaborate. The County Councils had to consult District and Parish Councils and then prepare draft map and accompanying statements describing the paths and ways. Notice was then given by public advertisement and objections could then be made by landowners. Determination of the objections then took place and this was followed by the preparation of a provisional map and statement and again there was allowance for objections to be heard. Only after this process was completed was the County Council able to publish the Definitive Map and Statement.

Reviews

The National Parks and Access to the Countryside Act 1949 allowed for periodic reviews of the Draft Map and Statement to take account of developments since the original survey or previous review. The developments would include the discovery of information which suggested that a path or way had been wrongly omitted from the definitive map and statement, new footpaths and bridleways which had come into existence as the result of dedication, creation agreements and orders and the extinguishment of paths or ways following extinguishment and diversion orders. The review was also to show changes of status such as a footpath becoming a bridleway etc.. The reviews were to be on a county-wide basis and were to be undertaken at intervals of not more than five years. The procedure was almost as cumbersome as that for the original definitive map and Statement.

Modification Orders

This process of review was changed initially by the *Countryside Act 1968* which made the process of review rather less cumbersome, although still requiring reviews every five years.

More radically, the process of review was further changed by the *Wildlife and Countryside Act 1981* which abolished the system of countywide reviews and replaced it with modification orders which could be made at any time. Under this system, the surveying authorities have the duty of keeping the definitive map and statement up to date as and when changes occur by way of modification orders.

The highway authorities are specifically required to make modification order to reflect the occurrence of the following events[1]:

1. a highway shown or required to be shown in the definitive map and statement has been authorised to be stopped up, diverted, widened or extended;
2. a highway shown or required to be shown in the definitive map and statement as a highway of a particular description has ceased to be a highway of that description;
3. a new right of way has been created over land in the area to which the map relates, being a right of way such that the land over which the right subsists is a public path;
4. the expiration of any period in relation to which the use by the public of that way raises a presumption that the way has been dedicated as a public path;
5. the discovery of evidence which (when considered together with all other relevant evidence) shows:
   – that a right of way subsists
   – that a right of way shown in the definitive map and statement as being of one description should be shown as being of another description;
   – that a public right of way shown in the map and statement should not be shown as a highway of any description;
   – that other particulars contained in the map and statement require modification.

This process of continuous review by the surveying authorities is supplemented by the right of any person to apply to the surveying authority

---

[1] s 53 of the Act

for a modification order. Such applications may be made on the basis that one of the occurrences set out under 4 and 5 above pertain.

Direction by Secretary of State
If the surveying authority fails to make a decision as to whether there should be a modification of the order, the applicant may make representations to the Secretary of State for a direction that the application be determined within a specified period.

If the surveying authority decides not to make an order, the applicant may appeal against the decision. The procedure is set out in paragraph 4 of Schedule 14 of the Highways Act 1980.

Reclassification of Rupps

The Countryside Act 1968 also required the reclassification of Rupps. The significance of this for footpaths and bridleways was that in effect there was a presumption that a way which had been shown as a Rupp was a bridleway and would not be shown as a footpath unless there was positive evidence to the effect that the rights were limited to pedestrians.

Under the Wildlife and Countryside Act 1981, the requirement to reclassify rights of way shown in the definitive map and statement as Rupps was re-enacted and the following approach to the reclassification of Rupps was stipulated:

- If a public right of way for vehicular traffic had been shown to exist then the way would be reclassified as a byway open to all traffic.
- In all other cases the Rupp would be classified as a bridleway unless bridleway rights had been shown not to exist.
  In other words all Rupps should be reclassified as bridleways unless there was positive evidence that either there were vehicular rights or that there were only pedestrian rights.

Inner London
Inner London is exempted by section 58 of the Wildlife and Countryside Act from the requirement for a Definitive Map.

Ordnance Survey maps

The routes shown on the definitive maps are shown on the Ordnance Survey maps on the scales 1:25,000, 1:50,000 and 1:63,000 (known as one inch or Tourist maps). The 1:25,000 is particularly useful to users of footpaths and bridleways as it shows the field boundaries. The maps have separate markings for footpaths, bridleways, Rupps and byways open to all traffic.

Lists of footpaths and bridleways

In additions to its obligations to keep the definitive map and statement, the highway authority must keep a list of all the highways in their area which are maintainable at the public expense.[2]

Marking of Paths and Ways on the Ground

Signposts

Section 27 of the Countryside Act 1968 contains powers for highway authorities to erect and maintain signposts along any footpath or bridleway. In addition to this general power there is also a general duty (except in particular circumstances) to erect and maintain a signpost where a footpath and bridleway leaves a metalled road. The signpost must indicate that the public path is a footpath or bridleway and "so far as the highway authority consider convenient and appropriate" where the footpath and bridleway leads and the distance to any places named on the signpost.[3]

Signposts for strangers

It is also provided that it shall be the duty of the highway authority in exercise of their powers under the section to erect such signposts as may in the opinion of the highway authority be required to assist persons unfamiliar with the locality to follow the course of a footpath or bridleway.

Other persons may erect signposts along a footpath or bridleway, but they must obtain the permission of the highway authority[4] (otherwise such a signpost may constitute an obstruction). In exercising its powers under section 27 the highway authority must consult with the owner of the land over which the footpath and bridleway runs.[5]

Misleading notices

It is an offence for any person to place or maintain on or near any way shown on a definitive map as a footpath and bridleway a notice containing any false or misleading statement likely to deter the public from using the way.[6]

[2] s 36(6)
[3] s 27(2)
[4] See s 27(5)
[5] s 27(1)
[6] National Parks and Access to the Countryside Act 1949, s 57

Marking of paths and ways over arable land

Many footpaths and bridleways are situated on land which is under cultivation for at least part of the year. Such paths may be difficult to identify if they are not specifically marked. If the line of the path is actually under cultivation users may be reluctant to use the path, not knowing whether they are taking precisely the right line whilst knowing that they are doing damage to crops. They may also find it physically difficult to walk along a path which has been ploughed. At the same time the existence of a footpath and bridleway across arable land may make it difficult and expensive for a farmer to plough his land without interfering with the line of the path.

The legal solution to these problems is provided by section 134 of the Highways Act.[7] This section provides that in the case of a cross-field footpath or bridleway, the owner or occupier of the land will have the right to plough or otherwise disturb the surface of the path. He only has this right however where the desire to disturb the path is in accordance with the rules of good husbandry and it is not reasonably convenient to avoid the disturbance.

Making good the surface

However where the farmer exercises this right, he must within the relevant period make good the surface of the path or way to not less than its minimum width so as to make it reasonably convenient for the exercise of the right of way. In addition he must so indicate the line of the path or way on the ground to not less than its minimum width that it is apparent to members of the public wishing to use it. The relevant period is 14 days in relation to new crops and 24 hours otherwise.

If he fails to comply with the requirement as to reinstatement of the path or way, he commits an offence.

Marking on the ground

Where a footpath or bridleway runs across or adjacent to cultivated land, there is further help to the user of the path or way in the form of section 137A of the Highways Act. This states that where a crop other than grass has been sown or planted on agricultural land the occupier of the land must ensure that the footpath and bridleway is marked on the ground to its minimum width and must prevent the crops from encroaching on the path or way. Again, failure by the farmer to comply with this requirement is a criminal offence.

---

[7] As substituted by the Rights of Way Act 1990

Maintenance and Improvement

CHAPTER 5

Maintenance and Improvement

Role of the Highway Authority

We have seen that the traditional method of creating highways was by dedication and acceptance. At the same time there was at common law a presumption that a highway would be maintainable by the inhabitants at large. In other words, in accepting the highway that had been dedicated the public thereby assumed responsibility for the maintenance of it.

There were certain exceptions to this rule whereby in special circumstances the owner of the land over which the highway ran was regarded as having assumed responsibility for the maintenance of the highway. These circumstances are known as special enactment, tenure, prescription and enclosure. They are very limited in number, and are not sufficiently important to describe in detail in a work of this size. It may suffice to say that the least uncommon example would probably be that of prescription where the occupier and his predecessors have repaired and maintained the highway time out of mind.

Publicly maintainable paths and ways

Section 47 of the *National Parks and Access to the Countryside Act 1949* made all footpaths and bridleways in existence at that time or coming into being thereafter maintainable at the public expense. (In the case of paths and ways which up until then had been maintainable by individuals by reason of special enactment, tenure, prescription or enclosure the individuals would still have a liability to maintain and would have to pay for work executed by the highway authority even though the path or way became maintainable at the public expense.) This provision was repealed by the Highways Act 1959. However the position was maintained with regard to footpaths and bridleways which existed as at 31 December 1959. As regards footpaths and bridleways coming into existence after 31 December 1959, they would be maintainable at the public expense if they were dedicated under a public path order or agreement or in accordance with some other statutory procedure. In other cases there would be no person who incurred liability to repair. However a footpath or bridleway created by dedication after 31 December 1959 may still become maintainable at the public expense in a number of ways.

Section 37

Firstly the path or way may become maintainable at the public expense as the result of the procedure under section 37 of the Highways Act. Under this section, a person who proposes to dedicate a way as a highway and who desires that the proposed highway shall become maintainable at the public expense may serve a notice on the prospective highway authority for the way. If then the way is certified by the highway authority to have been dedicated in accordance with the notice, and made up in a satisfactory manner, and is then used as a highway for the ensuing 12 months and is kept by the landowner in repair for that time, the highway becomes maintainable at the public expense. However if the highway authority regard the way as not being of sufficient public utility, they may make a complaint to a magistrates' court for an order to that effect. If the council wrongly refuses to issue a certificate, the owner of the land may apply to a magistrates' court to compel it to do so.

Adoption

Secondly the highway authority may adopt the footpath or bridleway after its creation by agreement with the landowner.

Maintenance work

Thirdly, if the highway authority at any time undertake the maintenance of the footpath or bridleway the courts will readily infer that the highway has become publicly maintainable.

The upshot of these provisions is that the vast majority of foo' ~ths and bridleways are maintainable at the public expense. The Highways Act 1959 abolished the duty on the inhabitants at large to maintain highways, and imposed on highways authorities a duty to maintain those highways which are maintainable at the public expense. The result is that virtually all footpaths and bridleways are maintainable by the highway authority.

Dual responsibility

As we have seen, the fact that the highway authority has the duty to maintain a highway does not necessarily mean that no one else has the duty to maintain it. Where an individual was liable for maintenance of a highway before 1949, the duty imposed by section 47 of the National Parks and

Access to the Countryside Act 1949 did not discharge his liability.[1] In relation to footpaths and bridleways which are publicly maintainable and which the landowner is still under a duty to repair by virtue of special enactment, or tenure, enclosure or prescription, the position is made clear by section 57 of the Highways Act. This enables the highway authority for the highway to repair it and to "recover the necessary expenses of doing so from that person in any court of competent jurisdiction". However the person liable to maintain the path or way must be given the stipulated notice of repair by the highway authority, and must be given the opportunity to repair the path or way himself. In relation to those few footpaths and bridleways which are not maintainable at the public expense, the highway authority may nonetheless carry out proper repairs[2] and recover the expense from any person who is liable to maintain, subject to the provisions as to notice.

The Power to Maintain – other Authorities

Although the highway authority has the duty to maintain highways maintainable at the public expense, other persons or bodies may maintain such highways.

District Councils

Section 42
Non-metropolitan District Councils may undertake the maintenance of footpaths and bridleways in their area by way of two separate provisions. Section 42 of the Highways Act enables non-metropolitan District Councils to undertake the maintenance of certain highways in its area, including the footpaths and bridleways which are maintainable at the public expense. In order to exercise its powers under section 42, the District Council must give notice to the highway authority under the provisions of Schedule 17 to the Highways Act. District Councils can then claim reimbursement from the County Council of their expenses of maintaining the footpaths and bridleways. The procedure for submitting of estimates and recovering expenses is set out in Schedule 7.

The Schedule also makes provision for the District Council to indemnify the highway authority in respect of claims against the authority for failure

[1] See s 56 of the 1949 Act
[2] s 57(2)

to maintain whilst the powers of maintenance were being exercised by the District Council and for claims arising out of works of maintenance carried out by the District Council. The District Council stands in the shoes of the County Council in the discharge of the County Council's responsibilities. The County Council remains responsible under section 41 for the maintenance of publicly maintainable highways in its area, and the District Council is also liable in tort for both misfeasance and non-feasance.

Agency Agreements

The other provision whereby District Councils may undertake the maintenance of footpaths and bridleways in their area is by way of an "Agency Agreement" with the County Council. Such agreements are made possible by section 101 of the Local Government Act 1972. Usually such agency agreements provide for the discharge of wider functions by the District Councils than the maintenance provided for under section 42, otherwise it would be simpler to simply give a notice under section 42.

Parish and Community Councils

Under section 43 of the Highways Act parish and community councils have the right to maintain footpaths and bridleways in their areas which are maintainable at the public expense. Their right to maintain footpaths and bridleways does not eclipse the duty of the highway authority (or other person) to maintain the paths and ways. There is no obligation on highway authorities to reimburse parish or community councils for undertaking this maintenance. However highway authorities may defray part or all of any such expenditure, as may District Councils which have taken powers under section 42 in respect of the highways concerned.

Multiple maintenance

From the above we can see that there may be three legal persons who are liable for the maintenance of a footpath or bridleway, namely the highway authority, the District Council which has used its powers under section 42 and the landowner who is liable by reason of special enactment, tenure, prescription or enclosure. Additionally the footpaths and bridleways may be maintained by parish or community councils.

Whether this multiplicity of potential maintainers is useful is open to question. Certainly, implementation of section 42 powers and agency agreements are sometimes criticised on the grounds that the existence of more than one body having responsibility for the state of highways in an area causes confusion in the minds of the public.

The Nature of the Duty to Maintain

No standard of repair is laid down in the Highways Act and at common law there are two strands of authority which do not appear to have entirely blended with one another. The first is the principle that when a highway is dedicated, the public must take it as they find it.

Cooper v Walker [1862] 2 B&S 770
Where there is an erection or excavation upon land, and the land on which it is located, or to which it is contiguous, is dedicated to the public as a highway, the dedication must be taken to be made to the public and accepted by them, subject to the inconvenience or risk arising from the erection or excavation. In an action for a declaration that the defendant had negligently and improperly placed in a public street certain steps, so that the same were an obstruction to persons using the street, and dangerous to persons passing along it at night, and averring that the plaintiff fell over it and was injured; it was contended that the street was subject to the right of the occupier of the house adjoining the street to have steps standing in the highway and leading up to the outer door of the house. The steps had been replaced when the street had been lowered.

It was held that the former highway was subject to the right on the part of the occupiers of the defendant's house to keep the steps there and the lowered highway was subject to a similar right.

The way may also be dedicated subject to limitations and conditions. For example a way can be dedicated as a highway even though it be impassable in winter. The Wildlife and Countryside Act recognises that dedications may be subject to conditions and limitations by requiring the statements accompanying the definitive map to include particulars of limitations and conditions.[3]

The changing standard
The second strand of authority is the tendency of the courts to find that the level of repair which is required of the person who has the duty to maintain is determined by the ordinary use which is being made of the highway at the time when the level of repair comes into question. Thus, in the case of *R v Henley (Inhabitants)*, 1847 11 JPJ 804 the issue was whether the road was in a sufficient state of repair for the current use of it, and not by

[3] s 56(4)(b)

reference to its past condition. And in *Chichester Corporation* v *Foster* [1906] 1 KB 167 Lord Alverstone said:

> "It seems to me that *Att-Gen* v *Scott* is a distinct authority for the proposition that it is their duty to alter the standard of a road from time to time, as the traffic upon it becomes larger or alters its character. Such cases present great practical difficulties and I always direct juries on the basis that the standard of a road authority's duty must vary from time to time as the traffic becomes greater and more burdensome."

In *Birmingham Navigation Co* v *Attorney-General* [1915] AC 654 at 665 it was said:

> "It is the duty of road authorities to keep their public highways in a state fit to accommodate the ordinary traffic which passes or may be expected to pass along them. As the ordinary traffic expands or changes in character, so must the nature of the maintenance and repair of the highway alter to suit the change."

Whilst these two strands, the public being required to take a highway as they find it, and the level of maintenance being variable according to use, may not strictly conflict, there will evidently be situations where there is a tension between the two principles.

Of course, many of the cases which decided that the standard of maintenance rises as the highway becomes used by a greater volume of traffic were decided in relation to carriageways which were no doubt becoming subjected to greater traffic partly at least as the result of the advent of the motor car. Precisely the same principles apply to footpaths and bridleways on account of their status as highways.

However, for many footpaths and bridleways the situation during the present century has been the reverse, namely that they have become less frequented. By their nature they have not become frequented by different types of traffic (except for the use of bicycles on bridleways). Therefore it may seem that the above discussion is largely academic in relation to footpaths and bridleways. However there are footpaths and bridleways which do attract increased use where the requirement of the highway authority will be to cater for the demands which are currently made of the path or way.

There does not seem to be any reason for believing that the standard of maintenance becomes higher when a highway is publicly maintainable, but in reality that may be the case.

Enforcement of the responsibility to maintain

Under the provisions of section 56 of the Highways Act, a person may serve a notice on a highway authority requiring the authority to state whether they admit that the way is a highway and that they are liable to maintain it. Following the service of that notice, and depending on the response to it the complainant who serves the notice may then bring proceedings in the Magistrates' or Crown Court in order so secure the proper repaid by the highway authority of the way. If it is found that the way is a publicly maintainable highway and the highway authority is ordered to repair it, then if the highway remains unrepaired the complainant may secure a further order authorising the complainant to carry out the repairs and recover the cost from the highway authority.

Liability of the Highway Authority

Section 41 of the Highways Act, which imposes on the highway authority the duty to maintain highways maintainable at the public expense imports civil liability and the defence of "non-feasance" is no longer available. At common law the "inhabitants at large" could be made to put a highway into a state of proper repair by the sanction of being indicted at Quarter Sessions. However in a civil action for damages, the highway authority or its predecessor could rely upon the defence that the defect was caused by non-feasance as opposed to misfeasance. That defence was removed by section 1(1) of the Highways (Miscellaneous Provisions) Act 1961.

Statutory defence
There is a statutory defence which is available to a highway authority under section 58 of the Highways Act.

This section provides that it is a defence for the highway authority to prove that the authority had taken such care as in all the circumstances was reasonably required to secure that the part of the highway in question was not dangerous to traffic. Subsection (2) provides that in considering such a defence the court shall have regard to the following matters:

- the character of the highway in question and the traffic which was reasonably to be expected to use it;
- the standard of maintenance appropriate to a highway of that character, and used by such traffic;
- the state of repair in which a reasonable person would have expected to find the highway;

- whether the highway authority knew or could reasonably be expected to know that the condition of the part of the highway to which the action relates was likely to cause danger to users of the highway;
- where the highway authority could not reasonably have been expected to repair that part of the highway before the cause of action arose, what warning notices of its condition had been displayed.

It is also provided that it is not relevant for the highway authority to prove that it instructed a competent person to maintain the highway unless it is also proved that the highway authority had properly instructed him and that he had carried out the instructions.

Whiting v Hillingdon LBC (1970) 68 LGR 437

The plaintiff had stepped off a footpath and injured her leg on a tree stump hidden in the foliage which projected over the footpath. She brought an action against the highway authority under section 44(1) of the Highways Act 1959 (the predecessor of section 41) and for negligence and breach of duty under the Occupier's Liability Act 1957. The accident took place in April 1966. The footpath had been inspected in the summers of 1964 and 1965 and again in December 1965 and had been repaired in February 1966. However the inspections did not reveal the existence of the tree stump. The plaintiff contended that the annual inspections were not sufficient, but the judge rejected this submission, and said that it was not incumbent on the highway authority to beat the foliage to ensure that there was no hidden danger.

Tarrant v Rowlands and Another [1979] RTR 144

This was a carriageway case, where it was held that the highway authority was liable in respect of the accumulation of water at a place where water was known to flood the road and constituted a danger to traffic. The same would clearly apply to footpaths and bridleways.

Haydon v Kent County Council [1978] QB 343

The plaintiff slipped on a metalled footpath covered with impacted snow and ice and broke her ankle. She sued the Kent County Council for breach of duty under the equivalent of section 41 for breach of duty to maintain the path. The Court of Appeal held that since "maintenance" was held to *include* repair the duty was wider than the repair of the surface of the path itself and included the removal of snow and ice so as to keep the path safe for those not in breach of its duty. However to succeed in such an action, the plaintiff must show that there has a been a blameworthy neglect on the part of the highway authority.

On the facts of the case the court found that the Kent County Council had not been in breach of duty. It had a policy of treating main roads first and then those paths which were reported to the Kent County Council as dangerous. On the day in question the County Council had been told of the condition of the path in the morning and had had it cleared in the afternoon, but too late to prevent the accident.

Pure economic loss
Breach of the duty to maintain does not give rise to damages for pure economic loss (*Wentworth* v *Wiltshire County Council* [1993] 2 WLR 175.

Joint inspections following accidents
In the case of *Westphal* v *Haringey Borough Council*, reported in Circular "Roads 57/72" Cumming-Bruce J stressed the importance of joint inspections by the plaintiff and his legal representative and the highway authority following serious accidents on the highway. Such an inspection is aimed at agreeing the location of the accident and relevant measurements. Such a recommendation is of course subject to any necessity that may exist for urgent repair.

Paths and ways which cross railway lines
Many footpaths and bridleways which cross railway lines are the responsibility of the railway company or board under the *Railway Clauses Consolidation Act 1845*. Section 61 of that Act makes it the responsibility of the company to "make and maintain convenient ascents and descents and other convenient approaches, with handrails or other fences and ... good and sufficient gates ... and ... [in the case of a footpath] gates or stiles."

Section 61 applies only if the original Act authorising the construction of the line applied the Railway Clauses Consolidation Act.

Improvement

Part V of the Highways Act gives highway authorities and other persons numerous powers to improve highways by various different methods.

Many of these powers either specifically relate to carriageways or else are unlikely to be of importance in relation to footpaths and bridleways. Below are the provisions which are most likely to have relevance to paths and ways.

Section 62 introduces this part of the Act with a residual power given to highway authorities to improve highways generally in ways not covered by the specific provisions found in particular sections of this part. The power is to carry out "any work (including the provision of equipment) for the improvement of the highway."

Footbridges

Section 70 allows for the construction and maintenance of footbridges over highways for making the crossing less dangerous and easier for pedestrians or for protecting the traffic along the highway from danger.

Prevention of access

Section 80 allows for the erection, maintenance, alteration and removal of fences and posts to prevent access to a publicly maintainable highway (however this does not include the right to obstruct an established means of access or any means of access permitted under Town and Country Planning provisions). The means whereby a highway authority may stop up a private access to a highway are dealt with in sections 124–129. However the general powers of improvement do seem to encompass the power to interfere with rights of access (Lord Radcliffe in *Ching Garage* v *Chingford Corporation* [1961] 1 WLR 470) although this will be subject to compensation – as to which see below.

Marking the boundaries

Section 81 allows for the marking of the boundary of a highway with posts or stones.

Cattle grids

Sections 82–90 allow for the provision and maintenance of cattle grids.

Bridges

Sections 92–95 allow for the reconstruction and improvement of bridges.

Lighting

Sections 97 and 98 allow for the lighting by the highway authority of a publicly maintainable highway and for the delegation by the highway authority of its lighting functions to a lighting authority, that is, a council or other body authorised to provide lighting under section 161 of the Public Health Act 1875 or section 3 of the Parish Councils Act 1957 or any corresponding local enactment. There are other specific provisions in this part of the Act for the provision of lighting. These provisions are of limited relevance to footpaths and bridleways except in urban areas.

Metalling
Section 99 allows for the metalling of a publicly maintainable highway.

Drainage
Section 100 allows for the provision and maintenance of drainage for a highway.

Ditches
Section 101 allows for the filling in of ditches and watercourses adjoining and lying near to a highway where such ditches and watercourses are a danger to users of the highway. It also allows for the replacement of such ditches with pipes. Provision is made for consultation with landowners.

Hazards of nature
Section 102 allows for the protection of highways from snow, flood, landslide and other hazards of nature.

Depth posts
Section 103 requires a highway authority to provide graduated depth posts or stones for any highway which is subject to flooding to any considerable depth.

Widening
This part of the Act also allows for the widening of a highway by the highway authority entering to a dedication agreement with the owner of the land required, or where the highway authority already owns the land, by appropriating the land for the widening of the highway. These provisions are contained in sections 62 and 65. There are provisions elsewhere in the Highways Act (Part XII) for the compulsory purchase of land for the widening of highways.

Compensation
In this part of the Act there are numerous provisions as to the payment of compensation to landowners where their land is affected by the improvements.

Powers of entry to execute works
Although the powers of improvement are wide, highway authorities may not always be able to take advantage of them. For example, if a publicly maintainable footpath bridge over a stream needs replacing, it may be impossible for the highway authority to get the necessary plant and equipment to the site of the work without the cooperation of the owner.

If, for example, the footpath is 1.8 metres wide, then the vehicles necessary to carry the plant and equipment may not be capable of being accommodated by the footpath. It may be physically impossible to drive the vehicle(s) along the footpath because of fences or hedges on each side or, even if it is physically possible, the landowner may not give permission for the vehicles to use the route, in which case the vehicles would be trespassing in order to reach the site of the bridge.

It is clear that the highway authority needs a power of entry on to the land in this type of situation.

There are provisions in the Highways Act for powers of entry onto land. Under Schedule 12A, the highway authority (or district council empowered under sections 42 and 50 of the Act) may enter on land for any purpose connected with the carrying out of work for making good the surface of a footpath or bridleway which has been so disturbed as to render it inconvenient for the exercise of the public right of way. The highway authority or district council have to give notice of the entry on to the land in compliance with the provisions of the Schedule.

The provision for entry by the highway authority also applies in the following circumstances:

- where the surface of the footpath or bridleway has been disturbed by a farmer under the provisions of section 134 (ploughing etc) but has not been made good within the time allowed; or
- where the farmer has carried out engineering or excavation operations with the permission of the highway authority under section 135 and has failed to reinstate it to the stipulation of the highway authority;
- where the farmer has allowed crops to obscure the line of a footpath or bridleway (s 137A(1)(a));
- where the farmer has failed to prevent crops encroaching onto a footpath or bridleway as to render it inconvenient for the exercise of the right of way (s 137A(1)(b)).

Section 291 of the Highways Act authorises the entry on land by the highway authority where the entry is necessary for the purpose of maintaining, altering, or removing any structure or work which is situated on over or under that land. It will be noted (with reference to the problem posed above) that there is no reference to "replacement" of a structure.

These powers of entry under the Highways Act are expressed to be in favour of a person duly authorised in writing by the relevant authority.

Entry to survey

Further, under section 293 powers of entry are given to highway and other relevant authorities for the purposes of surveying land and estimating its value for the purposes of claims for compensation payable in relation to a public path creation or extinguishment order, etc.

Under section 294, a highway authority or council which has been refused permission to enter, examine, or lay open any premises may make a complaint to a magistrates court for an order permitting the entry examination or laying open, where the highway authority or council show that they need the order for the purposes of:

– surveying
– making plans
– executing maintaining or examining works
– ascertaining the course of sewers or drains
– ascertaining or fixing boundaries
– ascertaining whether any hedge tree or shrub is dead, diseased, damaged or insecurely rooted.

This power is available only in relation to specified functions under the Highways Act. As regards footpaths and bridleways the power is available in relation to:

– filling in ditches (with or without laying pipes in them (s 101);
– the cutting or felling of overhanging trees (s 154(2));
– the keeping by highway authorities of lists of highways in their areas which are maintainable at the public expense (s 36(6));
– the adoption of a highway by agreement (s 38);
– provision or removal of barriers, rails, or fences for a public footpath (s 66(3) and (4));
– the cutting or lopping of hedges trees or shrubs which overhangs a highway so as to endanger or obstruct the passage of pedestrians (s 154);
– unfenced or inadequately fenced source of danger to persons using a street (which term, as we have seen includes footpaths and bridleways)(s 165);
– power of highway authority or council to require information as to the ownership of land (s 297).

Under section 71 of the Road Traffic Regulation Act 1984, an authority may enter land for the purpose of placing, replacing, converting and removing signposts and other signs or notices.

CHAPTER 6

Obstructions and Interference

CHAPTER 6

Obstructions and Interference

Obstructions of the highway and other interference with, or misuse of, the highway may be actionable under civil or criminal law both under common law and statute. Such is the status of a highway that obstructions will be easily regarded as a public nuisance even though there remains room for the public to pass and repass. It will be seen from the cases referred to below that the courts are not slow to infer that any interference with the use of the highway is actionable in some form and/or another.

Common Law

Under common law an obstruction of the highway without statutory authority is a nuisance and an indictable offence.

R v Clark [1963] 3 WLR 1067
The defendant was convicted after trial on indictment for obstructing the highway by leading a group of people around a police cordon so that they partially blocked one street and entirely blocked another.

On appeal it was held that the obstruction would have amounted to a nuisance at common law only if the user of the highway was unreasonable, (and since the jury had not been directed on unreasonableness the conviction was quashed).

Campbell v Paddington Corporation [1911] 1 KB 869
The plaintiff was in possession of a house from the windows of which there was an uninterrupted views of part of a main thoroughfare along which the funeral procession of Edward VII was to pass. The plaintiff arranged to hire out seats on her balcony for the time of the procession. The defendants caused a stand to be erected in the Edgeware Road (in which the plaintiff's house was situated) so that they and their friends could watch the procession. The erection of the stand made the plaintiff's balcony unlettable and she brought the action for the recovery of £90 damages to reflect her loss of profit.

It was held by the Court of Appeal that the erection of the stand was a public nuisance and that the plaintiff could recover her loss.

Even where the highway is wide, an obstruction will still be a nuisance even if only a small part of the highway is obstructed (*Nagy* v *Weston* [1965] 1 WLR 280 and *Brandon* v *Barnes* [1966] 1 WLR 1505).

Other nuisances. It is not only obstructions of the highway that constitute nuisances.

R v Clark (1883) 15 Cox, CC 171

The defendant was indicted for unlawfully exposing the dead body of her infant child near a public highway. The jury found that the exposure was calculated to shock and disgust passers-by. The defendant was found guilty of nuisance at common law.

Straying animals

Fitzgerald v E D and A D Cooke Bourne (Farms) [1963] 3 All ER 36

Two young unbroken fillies were kept by the owner for many months without complaint in a field across which ran a public footpath. As the plaintiff was walking along the footpath, the fillies galloped across the field from behind her, and got in front of her; one of them swerved around, and prancing about, struck her with its shoulder and knocked her down. She was badly frightened and suffered a nervous breakdown.

It was held that she was unable to claim damages, *inter alia*, on the ground that the animals were not known to have a vicious propensity. Diplock L J said that "the owner of domestic animals which are not known to him to be vicious, which are grazing on land on which he has a right to depasture them, owes no duty to a person exercising his right of using a highway which passes across or adjoining that land to take any steps to prevent their causing damage in the course of following the natural propensities of their kind."

As to statutory liability for animals see below.

Statutory nuisances

Part III of the *Environmental Protection Act 1990* requires local authorities to inspect their areas in order to detect statutory nuisances which require addressing. These statutory nuisances include the following:

- any premises in such a state as to be prejudicial to health or a nuisance;
- any accumulation or deposit which is prejudicial to health or a nuisance;
- any animal kept in such a place or manner as to be prejudicial to health or a nuisance.

Further, any person aggrieved by a statutory nuisance may apply to a magistrates court by way of a complaint. If the court is satisfied that the alleged nuisance exists or that, although abated, it is likely to recur on the same premises, the court shall make an order:

(a) requiring the defendant to abate the nuisance within a specified time and to execute any works necessary to prevent its recurrence; and/or

(b) prohibiting the recurrence of the nuisance and requiring the defendant to execute within a specified time any works necessary to prevent the recurrence.

This unusual provision enables magistrates' courts to issue what is in effect an injunction against causing or permitting statutory nuisances. Whilst there is no specific reference to the highway, the provision is clearly of considerable use for the prevention of nuisances on the highway.

Animals

The *Animals Act 1971* makes a keeper (who may or may not be the owner) liable for damage caused by an animal which is a member of a dangerous species and for animals of other species if either:

- the damage is of a kind which the animal unless restrained was likely to cause; or
- the damage of not of a kind which the animal unless restrained was likely to cause, but if the animal did do such damage it was likely to be severe;

and the keeper had knowledge (actual or to be imputed under the Act) of the characteristic of the particular animal which are not normally found in animals of the same species (or not normally found except at particular times and in particular circumstances). For the precise wording of this rather convoluted provision, the reader should refer to the Act.

Statutory offences

Part IX of the Highways Act deals with the lawful and unlawful interference with highways and streets. This part of the Act contains 55 sections which mainly deal with obstructions, encroachments, nuisances and interferences in the highway and gives the highway authorities powers to deal with these.

Section 130

This part of the Act starts with the very important section 130 which in subsection (1) places on highway authorities the duty to assert and protect the rights of the public to the use and enjoyment of the highways for which they are the authority.

In subsection (2) any council which is not a highway authority is empowered to assert and protect the rights of the public to the use and enjoyment of the of any highway in their area.

Subsection (3) places on a local highway authority the duty of preventing the stopping up or obstruction of highways for which they are the highway authority, and of other highways if in their opinion the stopping up or obstruction of that highway would be prejudicial to the interests of their area.

Subsection (5) gives a Council power to institute legal proceedings in their own name, defend any legal proceedings and generally take such steps as they deem expedient for the performance of their functions under section 130. This of course includes the right to apply for injunctions. In some cases where offenders persist in obstructing the highway even after they have been successfully prosecuted for doing so, there may be little point in the County (or other) Council continuing to prosecute for further similar offences. An injunction, with attendant powers of arrest and imprisonment for contempt of court may offer a better deterrent to the offender. However whichever course the council adopts it has to be prepared for a long drawn out battle with many returns to court if the offender intends to continue flouting the law (usually because it is profitable for him to do so).

Subsection (6) places a duty on a highway authority to take proper proceedings where a representation is made to them by a parish or community council (or parish or community meeting) to the effect that a highway has been unlawfully stopped up or obstructed or that an unlawful encroachment has taken place on roadside waste, unless the highway authority is satisfied that the representation is incorrect.

Offences
The remainder of this part of the Act contains a number of provisions which are of relevance to footpaths and bridleways. Most of them create offences for interference with the path or way. There follows a brief description of the more important offences which may be committed in relation to paths and ways. For these sections references to the local authority means different things in different contexts. Frequently it means the highway authority or the district council. In relation to a number of the offences the highway authority is given the power to remove the nuisance

and charge the cost to the offender in addition to the power of prosecution. In relation to some of the offences statutory defences are provided.

The following actions are prohibited.

removal of soil or turf
>section 131(1)(b): to remove any soil or turf from any part of a highway (except for the purpose of improving the highway with the consent of the highway authority);

deposits on a highway
>section 131(1)(c): to deposit any thing whatsoever on a highway so as to damage to the highway;

pulling down a milestone
>section 131(2): without lawful excuse to pull down or obliterate a milestone or direction post (but it is a defence to prove that it was not lawfully so placed);

disturbing the surface
>section 131A: to disturb the surface of a footpath or bridleway so as to render it inconvenient for the exercise of the public right of way;

affixing unauthorised marks
>section 132: to affix unauthorised marks on the surface of the highway or on any tree, structure or works on or in the highway;

ploughing up a path or way
>section 134: to plough up a footpath or bridleway unless certain requirements are observed.

(It appears to be a curiosity of this provision that no mention is made of situations where the footpath or bridleway is subject to the condition that the landowner has the right to plough. It may well be registered as such on the statement accompanying the definitive map. It would appear that a landowner who has dedicated a path or way subject to an unfettered right to plough will now find that he can only plough if he observes the conditions appearing in this section. On the face of it the offence enacted here seems to restrict that right to plough without compensation to the owner of the land.)

obstructing free passage
>section 137: wilfully to obstruct the free passage along a highway;

The meaning of the term "wilfully" was considered in:

Arrowsmith v Jenkins [1963] 2 QB 561

The defendant held a public meeting on a highway, resulting in the obstruction of the highway by those attending. She was prosecuted for wilfully obstructing the highway. She was convicted and appealed to quarter sessions on the basis that the prosecution had to show that she intended to obstruct the highway.

Her appeal was dismissed and it was held that where the defendant wilfully does an act which results in the obstruction of the highway she will be guilty of the offence.

It seems that prosecutions under this section, and indeed under some other sections within this part, may give rise to complex questions of right.

R v Ogden, ex p Long Ashton Rural District Council [1963] 1 All ER 574

The Rural District Council as highway authority prosecuted the defendant under the predecessor of this section for erecting a fence across a public right of way. The defendant admitted the obstruction but denied that there was a right of way. The justices declined to hear the prosecution on the ground that they lacked jurisdiction. The Divisional Court granted mandamus, so that the justices had to determine whether or not the footpath existed.

Other cases on obstruction include the following:

Attorney-General v Wilcox [1938] 3 All ER 367

The owner of land over which a tow path ran put up posts to stop motor cars, ice cream barrows and other vehicles from using it. A declaration was claimed against him to the effect that the posts were an obstruction and a public nuisance. On behalf of the defendant it was argued that the obstruction to lawful users of the path was trivial and in any event to their advantage as the exclusion of vehicles improved the amenity of pedestrians.

This proposition was accepted but it was held that the declaration would be granted as the posts could be dangerous if not lighted at night and would interfere with the right of towage.

Durham County Council v Scott, *The Times*, 28 May 1990

The erection of a gate across a bridleway could amount to an unlawful obstruction under this section.

Gates
Section 145: to fail to enlarge or remove a gate across the highway when required by notice to do so.

This section applies to bridleways but not to footpaths. Where there is a gate of less than five feet in width across a bridleway, the highway authority may by notice to the owner of the gate require him to enlarge it or remove it.

Deposits
Section 148(c): to deposit any thing whatsoever on the highway to the interruption of any user of the highway.

The term "deposit" was considered in:

Scott v Westminster City Council, *The Times*, 7 February 1995
The plaintiff was a street trader selling hot chestnuts from a brazier on wheels in Oxford Circus. Officers of the City Council seized the brazier as being deposited on the highway so as to constitute a danger under section 149. The plaintiff brought an action seeking the return of the brazier. The judge at first instance held that the brazier was not deposited on the highway since "deposit" has some connotation of extent in time, and connotes putting and leaving.

On appeal to the Court of Appeal, Lord Justice Waite said that the judge was wrong. The verb "to deposit" was a term of wide connotation apt to describe the placing of one object on another ... the braziers on their barrows stationed on the highway with attendants selling from them were to be regarded as "deposited" on the highway.

Overhanging vegetation
Section 154(1): to allow vegetation to overhang the highway after notice from the authority to lop it.

The wording is "where a hedge, tree or shrub overhangs a highway ... so as to endanger or obstruct the passage of vehicles or pedestrians ..." This appears to omit horses and equestrians.

Dangerous hedges
Section 154(2): to fail to cut or fell a hedge, tree or shrub which is dead, diseased, damaged or insecurely rooted, and likely to cause danger by falling on a highway where the occupier has been served with a notice by the competent authority.

Straying animals
Section 155: to allow animals to stray onto the highway.

> "If any horses, cattle, goats or swine are at any time found straying or lying
> on or at the side of a highway their keeper is guilty of an offence; but this
> does not apply to any part of a highway passing over any common, waste
> or unenclosed ground."

The fact that it is an offence under this section to allow animals to stray
on to the highway does not make it actionable in the civil courts. As regards
civil liability there is no duty to fence animals generally (*Goodwyn* v
Cheveley (1859) H&N 631). Civil liability does attach where an animal
causes damage or injury and either the animal was of a dangerous species
or the keeper was aware of the animal's tendency to cause damage or
injury (for the precise criteria see section 2 of the Animals Act 1971).

Dangerous and annoying deposits
Section 161: to deposit anything whatsoever on the highway (without lawful
authority or excuse) as a consequence of which a user of the highway is
injured or endangered or to commit certain other acts causing danger or
annoyance.

Ropes across highways
Section 162: to place a rope, wire or other apparatus across the highway in
such a manner as to cause danger to persons using it – unless the defendant
proves that he has taken all necessary means to give adequate warning of
the danger.

Water
Section 163: to allow water to flow onto a highway after notice from the
authority.

Overhead cables and wires etc.
Section 178: to fix or place any overhead beam, rail, pipe, cable wire etc over
along or across a highway without the consent of the highway authority.

CHAPTER 7

Stopping up and Diversion

Stopping up and Diversion

"Once a highway always a highway"

We have mentioned that there is an old common law principle that "once a highway always a highway". A highway might cease to exist by falling into the sea, but even in such a case it would have to be clear that the highway could not be reinstated at reasonable cost. The only way short of physical disappearance in which a highway can cease to exist is by closure after the implementation of one of the statutory procedures.

In addition to the procedures which are expressly aimed at extinguishment of footpaths and bridleways, diversions result in stopping up of parts of highways. As mentioned in Chapter 3, a diversion consists of two parts, a stopping up and the creation of the replacement section of highway. In that chapter there was reference to diversions in so far as they involved the creation of new paths or ways. In the present chapter emphasis will be placed on the stopping up aspect of diversions.

It will be seen that there are two types of extinguishment and diversions. The first type is where the extinguishment or diversion is ancillary to some other scheme or project such as the building of a new road or the implementation of a building development. The other type is where the stopping up or diversion is being promoted for intrinsic reasons such as disuse or the provisions of a more convenient way.

Side roads Orders

Reference has already been made to sections 14 and 18 of the Highways Act 1980 which make provision for the stopping up and diversion of highways which cross or join trunk roads, classified roads or special roads which are in existence or to be built. There are similar powers in relation to highways for which planning permission has been granted for construction or improvement. These powers are contained in section 248 of the Town and Country Planning Act 1990.

Part VIII of the Highways Act

This part of the Act makes further provision for the diversion and stopping up of highways.

Section 116
Section 116 of the Act provides:

> "... if it appears to a Magistrates' Court, after a view, if the Court thinks fit by any two or more of the justices composing the Court that a highway ...
>> (a) is unnecessary, or
>> (b) can be diverted so as to make it nearer or more commodious to the public, the Court may by Order authorise it to be stopped up or, as the case may be, to be so diverted."

The procedure under this section can only be initiated by the highway authority.

Giving notice
Provision is made for the giving of notices to the relevant district and parish councils, which have a right of veto.

Notice also has to be given to owners and occupiers of adjoining lands, to statutory undertakers with apparatus under the highway, in the *London Gazette*, and in at least one local newspaper. Notices have to be displayed in a prominent position at the ends of the highway.

Hearing
On the hearing of the application all the persons who have a right to be served with the notices, together with any person who uses the highway and any other person who would be aggrieved by the order have a right to be heard. If the magistrates make the order these people have a right of appeal to the Crown Court (whether or not they have appeared before the magistrates).

Consent of landowners
Where an order for a diversion is made, the written consent of every landowner over whose land the diversion is to lie must be obtained.

In making a stopping up or diversion order, the magistrates can reserve a right of way as footpath or bridleway so that the stopping up or diversion is limited in effect.

Although the application under section 116 is limited to highway authorities, another person may request the highway authority to make such an application and if it does so, the highway authority may require that person to make provision for the costs of the application.

Sections 118 and 119

Sections 118 and 119 provide quite different procedures for the stopping up of footpaths and bridleways. In this case, the Order is made by a County or District Council. The criterion for the stopping up or diversion is whether or not the stopping up or diversion is expedient. In the case of the stopping up under section 118, the question is whether it is expedient that the path should be stopped up on the ground that it is not needed for public use. In the case of a section 119 diversion the criterion is that of expedience in the interest of the owner or occupier of land.

However a section 118 stopping up order may only be confirmed when the highway authority is satisfied that it is expedient to make the order, having regard to the extent that the path would, apart from the order, be likely to be used by the public. Regard must also be had to the effect on land served by the path or way. A section 119 diversion order may only be confirmed if the new path will be "substantially as convenient" to the public in respect of the starting and finishing points, and if it is expedient to confirm the order having regard to the effect the diversion would have "on public enjoyment of the path or way as a whole".

In contrast to a section 116 Order, the landowners over whose land the proposed diversion is to run do not have to give their written consent to the proposed order, although of course such landowners have to be notified of the proposal to make the order.

Section 120

In section 120 there are provisions for the making of stopping up and diversion orders where the right of way in question lies within more than one administrative area. There are also reserve powers for the Secretary of State to make orders under section 118 and 119 where no council has made such an order.

Temporary diversions

Section 122 allows for the provision of a temporary diversion where a highway is being widened or repaired.

Procedures for the making of Orders under the Highways Act 1980

The procedure for making Orders under sections 118 and 119 is laid out in Schedule 6 which is the same Schedule as applies to public path creation Orders under section 26 of the Act. The authority making the Order must advertise the Order in a local newspaper. The published notice must state the general effect of the Order, must specify where the draft Order can be inspected and must state the time allowed for objections. The authority must also serve a copy of the notice and draft Order on specified persons including relevant owners occupiers and lessees, local authorities and parish and community councils. They must also display a notice at the ends of the highway proposed to be stopped up.

If there are objections, there are provisions for the holding of a local inquiry or hearing of the objection.

The procedure for making Side Roads Orders is contained in Schedule 1 of the Highways Act. Again there is extensive and detailed provision for the giving of notice, including the advertisement of the Orders, service of the notice on specified persons, and the displaying of the notice at the ends of any highway to be stopped up. If any objection is received from a person required to be served with the notice or any other person appearing to be affected by the Order, a local inquiry is to be held.

Orders under Part X of the Town and Country Planning Act 1990

This part of the Town and Country Planning Act allows for the making of Orders stopping up or diverting any highway where that highway is affected by development or runs over land which is being developed.

Under *section 247* of the Act the Secretary of State may by Order authorise the stopping up or diversion of any highway if he is satisfied that it is necessary to do so in order to enable development to be carried out in accordance with planning permission granted under Part III of the Act or by a government department.

Section 248 contains a provision which is similar to the Side Roads Orders provisions under sections 14 and 18 of the Highways Act. The section empowers the Secretary of State to authorise by Order the stopping up or diversion of a highway (the subsidiary highway) which crosses or enters the route of another (the main) highway for which planning permission is granted.

Under *section 251* of the Town and Country Planning Act where land has been acquired for planning purposes and is for the time being held by a local authority for the purposes for which it was acquired, the Secretary of State may by order extinguish any public right of way over the land if he is satisfied that an alternative right of way has been or will be provided; or that the provision of an alternative right of way is not required.

The Orders under Part X mentioned so far are Orders to be made by the Secretary of State. *Sections 257 and 258* allow for the making of Orders by local planning authorities. Under section 257 a council which grants planning permission may make a stopping up or diversion Order in relation to footpaths and bridleways if it is necessary to do so to enable the planned development to be carried out in accordance with the permission.

Under *section 258* a local authority which has acquired or appropriated land for planning purposes may make an Order extinguishing any footpath or bridleway if satisfied that a right of way will be provided or is not required.

Procedures under Part X

The procedures for making of Orders by the Secretary of State are set out in section 252. The Secretary of State is required to take steps in many respects similar to those under Schedule 6 of the Highways Act. He must advertise the Order in a local newspaper and in the *London Gazette*, and the published notice must state the general effect of the Order, must specify where the draft Order can be inspected and must state that any person may object.

He must also serve a copy of the notice and draft Order on relevant local authorities and on specified statutory undertakers. He must display a notice at the site of the highway proposed to be stopped up. If there is any objection, he must cause a local inquiry to be held, unless the objection is made by a person other than a local authority or statutory undertaker, and he is satisfied that a public inquiry is not necessary. In certain circumstances the Order must be dealt with by special parliamentary procedure.

This procedure is unusual in that there is no requirement for the notification of owners onto whose land the way is to be diverted or for compensation.

The procedure for Orders made by local planning authorities under sections 257 and 258 is set out in Schedule 14 to the Act. The provisions as to advertisement and the displaying of notices are similar to those in respect of Orders made by the Secretary of State. Notice must also be given to the same persons as must be notified by the Secretary of State, with some additions, including all owners, occupiers and lessees of the land to which the Order relates. However the Secretary of State may direct in particular cases that such notices need not be served on owners (unless the owner is a local authority or statutory undertaker).

Inquiries and confirmation

Again, there are provisions for the holding of public inquiries if there are objections to the proposed Orders by any local authority. If there are other objections, then they will be dealt with by either a local inquiry or a hearing by an "appointed person" or inspector as they are more usually called. If there are objections then the Order will have to be confirmed by the Secretary of State after the inquiry or hearing. If there are no objections, then the Order-making authority may itself confirm the order.

Compensation

Provisions are also made for compensation of landowners for depreciation or disturbance. In relation to diversion and extinguishment orders under section 118 and 119 of the Highways Act the compensation is dealt with under sections 121 and section 28.

Other procedures

Whilst the most commonly used procedures for stopping up and diversion are those under the Highways Act followed by those under the Town and Country Planning Act, there are a number of other statutory procedures. The statutes which provide these procedures are the following:

Defence Acts of 1842 and 1860
Military Lands Act 1892
Lands Powers (Defence Act) 1958
Local Government Planning and Land Act 1980
Acquisition of Land Act 1981
New Towns Act 1981
Civil Aviation Act 1982
Cycle Tracks Act 1984
Housing Acts 1985 and 1988
Airports Act 1986
Water Act 1989.

CHAPTER 8

Remedies

CHAPTER 8

Remedies

There are many different types of dispute which arise in relation to footpaths and bridleways: abuse of the rights of those who have an interest in footpaths and bridleways; disputes as to the extent or existence of those rights; accidents and so on. In this chapter we look at the main remedies which are available to those aggrieved in relation to such problems. Once again we will look at the various remedies of the three main interests.

Remedies of the Landowner

Where he disputes the right of way

Where a landowner disputes that a way over his land is a public right of way, he may take direct action to prevent people from using it, or he may initiate various procedures to clarify the situation.

Direct action

Assuming that the putative right of way is not shown on the definitive map, the landowner may prohibit or prevent people coming on to the land. Either of these actions will constitute an act which brings the right of way into question for the purposes of the 20 year period in section 31 of the Highways Act. This may provoke an application to the highway authority by users of the highway for a Modification Order to add the path or way to the definitive map or other action to clarify the status of the way.

If he is not sure of the status of the way the landowner may find it more prudent to erect a notice than to put up a physical barrier to use of the way. If he erects a barrier, he may be prosecuted by the highway authority if the highway authority believes that the way is a public right of way, or the highway authority may seek an injunction against the landowner.

An alternative would be to close the way, perhaps by means of a gate or bar, for a certain period of each year. Preferably this should be accompanied by a permanent notice to the effect that the way will be barred at that time.

Legal or formal procedures

Declaration
The landowner may apply to the court for a declaration that the way is not a public right of way.

Lodging a map and statement
He may lodge with the local highway authority a map of his land and accompanying statement to the effect that there are no public rights of way over his land (or, where there exist other rights of way over his land) no rights of way other than those shown on the plan). This lodging will have the effect of constituting evidence to the effect that he does not have the intention to dedicate the way as a highway.

Application for modification
Of course, if the footpath or bridleway is already shown on the definitive map, the landowner's options are restricted. It would in those circumstances be illegal to take direct action, since the inclusion of the right of way in the definitive map would be conclusive proof of its status as shown. Realistically the best method by which a landowner can dispute the right of way in these circumstances is to apply to the highway authority under section 53(5) for a modification order on the basis that there is no right of way as shown in the map.

Preventing abuse
Where a landowner believes that a right of way over his land is being abused, he may threaten or commence an action in trespass against someone whom he suspects of the abuse, perhaps an habitual user. Again, this course carries risk in terms of potential costs if the landowner has any doubts about his cause.

Mayhew v Wardley (1863) 14 CBSN
Where the appellant and another man were seen standing on a highway and looking through a hole in the hedge, no-one else being near, and a gun was heard to be fired, and a dead partridge recently killed was found in the adjoining field within 18 yards of the hedge, it was held that the magistrates were correct in convicting the appellant for unlawfully committing trespass on the highway.

See also the discussion of the civil case of *Hickman* v *Maisey* in Chapter 2.

It follows that he may also require the trespasser to leave and, if he fails to do so, to evict him (*Harrison* v *Duke of Rutland*) – although if he reentered along the path or way without showing any signs on his return of abusing the right of way, presumably he could not be turned off a second time.

The right to remove objects placed on the highway

The owner of the soil of a highway may remove anything on the highway which is not consistent with (or, presumably, justified by) the right of way, even if it is not a nuisance (*R* v *Mathias* (1861) 2 f & f 570 NP). It is not clear, because of the age of this case, whether this applies to the owner of the subsoil (the landowner) as well as to the highway authority. It is presumed that it does, once again in accordance with the cases on trespass to the highway discussed in Chapter 2.

Remedies of the Highway Authority

Where a highway authority becomes aware of the abuse of or interference with a right of way, from any source, it will be obliged, by reasons of the duties imposed by section 130 of the Highways Act, to consider what action it should take to protect the rights of the public to enjoy the path or way.

Prosecutions

A highway authority which is faced with abuse of or interference with a right of way which is stipulated in Part IX of the Highways Act may initiate a prosecution under the relevant section of that part. The various offences are set out in Chapter 6.

Injunctions

A county council has the right to initiate proceedings in their own name where they consider it expedient for the promotion or protection of the interests of the inhabitants of their area under section 222 of the Local Government Act 1972 in addition to the authority given under section 130(5) of the Highways Act. See also the discussion below under **Which action is appropriate?**

Application for a declaration

Where the highway authority is unsure as to what is the legal status of a right of way or as to the existence of conditions or limitations which do not appear in the statement accompanying the definitive map, it may apply to the court for a declaration.

Serving notices to remove obstructions

Section 143 of the Highways Act empowers local highway authorities (and, where appropriate other competent authorities) to serve a notice requiring the removal of a structure which has been set up or erected on a highway otherwise than in accordance with statutory authority. The notice has to be served on the person having control or possession of the structure.

Direct action

Where a notice has been served under section 143 and the structure which is the subject of the notice has not been removed within a month from the service of the notice, the highway authority may remove the structure and recover the expense of doing so from the person having control or possession of the structure.

Barbed wire fences

Section 164 of the Highways Act deals with situations where there is a barbed wire fence on land adjoining a highway. The section empowers highway (and other competent) authorities to serve a notice on the occupier of land requiring him to abate the nuisance within a stipulated period being not less than one month or more than six months.

When is the highway authority required to act?

R v Lancashire County Council ex p Guyer [1980] 2 All ER 520

Landowners erected barriers over land which local residents claimed to be a footpath, although its existence was not shown on definitive maps. One of the residents sought an order of *mandamus* requiring the County Council to assert and protect the rights of the public under section 130. The order was refused. It was held that it was a matter of discretion for the County Council as to whether or not it instituted proceedings under section 130.

Which action is appropriate?

The choice of procedures open to highway authorities sometimes raises difficult questions. When faced, for example, with an obstruction or stopping up of a highway by a landowner the authority could seek an injunction against the landowner or prosecute (or make a modification order where appropriate). However where an action constitutes a criminal offence, as does obstruction of a highway, there is authority to say that the County Council should prosecute in the first instance rather than seek an injunction. (See *Stoke-on-Trent City Council* v *B & Q (Retail) Limited* [1984] 2 All ER 332.) Grant of an injunction is always discretionary and "a local authority should be reluctant to seek and the court should be reluctant to grant an injunction which if disobeyed may involve the infringer in sanctions far more onerous than the penalty imposed for the offence" (*Westminster City Council* v *Jones* [1981] JPL 750 DC). Further, the court may also in appropriate circumstances take into account the consideration that the Council does have alternative remedies open to it, such as making a modification order.

Under section 53 of the Wildlife and Countryside Act 1981, the surveying authority is under an obligation to keep the definitive map and statement under continuous review. This specifically includes the duty to make a modification order on the expiration of any period such that the enjoyment by the public of the right of way during that period raises a presumption that the way has been dedicated as a public path. If a landowner were prosecuted for obstructing a public footpath or bridleway and the path or way were not shown on the definitive map, the landowner would at the least be likely to attract some sympathy from the bench when he pointed to the duty on the surveying authority (who would as highway authority be the prosecutor) and the absence of the way on the definitive map.

In these circumstances a bench might be reluctant to impose a harsher penalty than a conditional discharge and might think carefully about ordering costs. The conservative approach on the part of the highway authority would surely in these circumstances be to go through the procedure of making a modification order before taking any other form of action.

Against this one has to remember that section 130 puts an onus on highway authorities to assert and protect the rights of the public to the use and enjoyment of highways, and that section 130(7) states that proceedings or steps taken by a council in relation to an alleged right of way are not to be treated as unauthorised by reason only that the alleged right of way is found not to exist.

R v Surrey County Council, ex p Send Parish Council (1979) 40 P & CR 390

Some frontagers had extended their gardens so as to block an alleged footpath or bridleway. The County Council eventually resolved to recognise the footpath to be included in the next definitive map (this was before the requirement of continuous review, enacted in the Wildlife and Countryside Act 1981). Notices were served under section 124 of the Highways Act 1959 (the predecessor of s 143), but no further action was taken until the Parish Council made a representation to the County Council under the predecessor of section 130(6). The frontagers then applied to the court for a Declaration that the path was not a footpath. The County Council did nothing to contest those proceedings. The Parish Council applied to the court for *mandamus* to compel the County Council to carry out its duty under the predecessor of section 130.

The court held that the County Council had failed to exercise its discretion under the Highways Act 1959. *Mandamus* was issued although it was left up to the County Council as to how exactly it would act. Lord Justice Lane said

> "The local authority must at all times act with the object of protecting the highway and of preventing or removing any obstruction, and more broadly speaking, of promoting the interests of those who enjoy the highway or should be enjoying the right of way and the county council must likewise operate against the interests of those who seek to interrupt such enjoyment of the highway."

Creation agreements, Orders, Diversion and Extinguishment Orders etc. In some situations the appropriate remedy to a dispute may be found in the creation, diversion or extinguishment of a path or way. These resources are dealt with in Chapters 2 and 7.

Remedies of District Councils

Taking action
Under section 130(2) of the Highways Act, District Councils may assert and protect the rights of the public to the use and enjoyment of any highway in their area for which they are not the highway authority. Under subsection (4) a District Council may in the performance of their function under subsection (2) institute legal proceedings in their own name, and take such other steps as they may deem expedient.

Remedies of parish and community Councils

Bringing pressure to bear on the highway authority
Under section 130(6) of the Highways Act, if the council of a parish or community or, in the case of a parish or community which does not have a separate parish or community council, the parish meeting or community meeting, represent to a local highway authority that a highway as to which the local highway authority have a duty under subsection (3) (that is the duty to prevent stopping up or obstruction) has been unlawfully stopped up or obstructed, it is the duty of the local highway authority, unless satisfied that the representations are incorrect, to take proper proceedings accordingly.

Remedies of the Public

Abatement
A member of the public who comes across an obstruction of a footpath and bridleway is normally entitled to remove it. This is discussed in Chapter 2.

Avoiding obstructions
Apart from the right of abatement a user of the footpath or bridleway may have the right to go off the path or way when he cannot go on along the line of the path or way on account of an obstruction. This is also discussed in Chapter 2.

Serving notice on the highway authority
Notices may be served on the highway authority under section 56 of the Highways Act to obtain action where any person wishes to complain that a highway maintainable at public expense is out of repair. Use of this procedure will result (where the highway authority disputes its liability) in a testing in the courts of whether the highway authority is obliged to repair the highway, or in enforcement in the courts of the duty to repair. See below under **Complaint to a magistrates' court**.

Taking proceedings against the highway authority

Mandamus
Where a highway authority fails to carry out its duties a person having an interest in the matter may apply to the High Court for an order of *mandamus* compelling the authority to perform its duty.

R v Lancashire County Council, ex p Guyer
The applicant sought to compel the County Council to institute proceedings under section 130 against landowners who had erected barriers over their land where a public right of way was claimed (although its existence was not shown on the definitive map.

Mandamus was refused on the basis that the County Council had a discretion whether to issue proceedings or not since the existence of the footpath was disputed. (See also *R v Surrey County Council, ex p Send Parish Council* [1979] 40 P & CR 390, above for a situation in which the County Council had failed to exercise its discretion correctly).

Application for a declaration
An individual whose interest is affected may apply to the court for a declaration in the same way as the highway authority.

Complaint to a magistrates' court
Section 56 of the Highways Act provides that where a person ("the complainant") alleges that a path or way is out of repair, he may serve a notice on the highway authority (or other person liable for the maintenance of the way) requiring the person served to state whether he admits that the way is a highway and that he is liable to maintain it. If within one month of the notice being served, the authority or person served does not serve on the complainant a notice admitting that the way is a highway and he is liable to maintain it, then the complainant may complain to the Crown Court for an order requiring the respondent to put the way in repair within a period specified in the order.

If the person served does admit that the way is a highway and that he is liable to maintain it, the complainant may then make a complaint to a magistrates' court for an order that the respondent put the highway in repair within a period specified in the order.

Section 150
Under section 150 of the Highways Act, if a highway authority has neglected to remove snow or soil from a highway, any person may make a complaint to a magistrates' court. If the complaint is proved, the court may order the highway authority to remove the obstruction within such period as it considers reasonable in all the circumstances.

Section 164
Where certain local authorities are the landowners in relation to land which is adjacent to the highway and that land has barbed wire on it which is a nuisance to the highway, any council tax payer may take proceedings under section 164 of the Highways Act.

Complaining to the Ombudsman
Where a highway authority or other council has failed to perform its duties under the Highways Act or other legislation, complaint may be made to the Commissioners or Local Ombudsmen set up under the Local Government Act 1974. The complaints procedure is intended for cases of maladministration, that is to say cases where the local authority have a clear duty to take action and fail to do so, or have delayed beyond a reasonable length of time etc. The ombudsman procedure is not intended for the resolution of disputes of fact or principle which could properly be dealt with by a court of law or other dispute resolution procedure.

Complaints may be made direct to the relevant Ombudsman or to the local authority in question and asking them to pass it on to the Ombudsman.

As the first step in the investigation of the complaint the Ombudsman will ask the Council concerned to comment on the complaint. The complaint may well be resolved at this stage. As a result of the complaints procedure the Ombudsman will report and make recommendations to the authority. He cannot force the authority to act, but local authorities usually comply with the Ombudsman's recommendations. The report has to be made available to the public and to the press.

CHAPTER 9

Inquiries

Inquiries

When a highway authority takes the view that a footpath or bridleway needs to be diverted or stopped up, or where it intends to make an order for the modification of the definitive map to show a footpath or bridleway which has not been recorded hitherto, there will frequently be opposition. Unless differences can be resolved by negotiation the upshot will very probably be a public inquiry. The purpose of the inquiry is to allow everyone who has an interest in the proposals to have their say so that the person making the decision is as well informed as possible as to the merits and defects of the scheme.

The inquiries which directly affect footpaths and bridleways are dealt with in various schedules to the relevant statutes. Inquiries under the provisions of Schedule 1 of the Highways Act relate to Side Roads Orders under sections 14 and 18 of the Highways Act. Inquiries into the making of orders solely relating to footpaths and bridleways come under the provisions of Schedule 6 of the Highways Act, Schedule 15 of the Wildlife and Countryside Act 1981 and Schedule 14 of the Town and Country Planning Act 1990.

Side Roads Order Inquiries

These Inquiries take place when a Side Roads Order is made, that is an Order for the stopping up, diversion, improvement or construction etc of a highway which crosses or enters the route of a special road, trunk or classified road which is in existence or to be built. There is no reason in principle why the main subject of such an order should not be a footpath or bridleway. However, many side roads orders involve substantial schemes for the construction of new stretches of trunk or classified road, and footpaths and bridleways are often only a small part of such Inquiries. For our purposes, any substantial discussion of Side Roads Order Inquiries would occupy a disproportionately large part of this book and will therefore be avoided.

However, for those readers who do become involved in Side Roads Order Inquiries, the following points may be of help:

The procedure as to the giving of notices, publication of the Inquiries, to be found in Schedule 1, have a great deal in common with the procedure for footpath or bridleway inquiries which are dealt with in this chapter.

It is extremely important to bear in mind the criterion contained in sections 14 and 18 of the Highways Act 1980. Subsection (6) of both sections 14 and 18 of the Highways Act 1980 contain the following words:

> "No order ... authorising the stopping up of a highway shall be made or confirmed by the Minister ... unless he is satisfied that another reasonably convenient route is available or will be provided before the highway is stopped up."

This is frequently the issue around which the battle rages in the part of Side Roads Order Inquiries which deals with footpaths and bridleways. There is a brief discussion of this issue in Chapter 3.

Footpath and Bridleway Inquiries

The following types of Order may give rise to a public Inquiry or a hearing:

- Public Path Creation Orders
- Public Path Extinguishment Orders
- Public Path Diversion Orders
- Agreements for the widening of a footpath or bridleway
- Certain Modification Orders.

The Modification Orders which will not give rise to a public inquiry are the Orders which result from a statutory procedure, namely a Public Path Creation Agreement or Order, Public Path Extinguishment Order and Public Path Diversion Order. That is, there is no requirement for a public inquiry where potential objectors have already had the opportunity to object and be heard, as where a Public Path Creation or Extinguishment Order gives rise to a Modification Order. This is something of a simplification but gives the gist of the provisions.

Where the making of an order is likely to affect interested parties who have not given their agreement or to give rise to disputes of fact, the legislation provides for the holding of an inquiry. The expiry of a period which is claimed to give rise to an inference of dedication, or the claim that a path or way shown on the definitive map should not be shown are typical such issues. These types of events are included within section 53(3) of the Wildlife and Countryside Act 1981. An inquiry will be held where there is any objection in relation to Orders which result from:

(a) the expiry of a period such that the enjoyment of the public by the way raises a presumption that the way has been dedicated as a public path;

(b) the discovery by the authority of evidence which shows:
  – that a right of way not shown in the definitive map subsists,
  – that a highway shown as one kind of highway (*e.g.* a bridleway) ought to be shown as a different kind of highway (*e.g.* a footpath), or
  – that there is no public right of way over land shown in the definitive map as a highway, or
  – that any other particulars in the definitive map and statement require modification.

Omnibus Orders

Where two or more Orders are proposed in relation to a small area of land or in relation to a particular group or network of paths and ways, it makes sense to make "omnibus orders" which contain more than one proposal. This enables the evidence to be heard on the separate proposals together and for a strategic view to be taken of the particular proposals.

Circular Roads No 2/93 states:

"The use of an omnibus order (*i.e.* one embracing several proposals within a local area) has a clear advantage over a single event order in terms of costs, and its use, wherever possible, is recommended."

Procedure

After the making of an Order by the highway or other appropriate authority, there are provisions for the giving of notices, and advertising, of the Order. Some details are given in Chapter 7.

Both Schedule 6 of the Highways Act 1980 and Schedule 15 of the Wildlife and Countryside Act 1981 allow for the placing of "standing orders" for the supply to individuals and groups of all creation, diversion, extinguishment and modification orders etc so that they do not have to keep a continual watch in the local press. A reasonable charge is payable.

In the case of modification orders there is an important addition to the normal requirement for the giving of notices and advertisement of the order. This is set out in paragraph 3(8) of Schedule 15 to the Wildlife and Countryside Act 1981:

> "At any time after the publication of a notice under this paragraph and before the expiration of the period specified in the notice for the making of representations and objections, any person may require the authority to inform him what documents (if any) were taken into account in preparing the order and –
>
>> (a) as respects any such documents in the possession of the authority, to permit him to inspect them and take copies; and
>>
>> (b) as respects any such documents not in their possession, to give him any information the authority have as to where the documents can be inspected;
>
> and on any requirement being made under this sub-paragraph the authority shall comply therewith within 14 days of the making of the requirement."

This provision is important as potential objectors will often have little if any idea of the evidence which was before the authority when they made up their mind to make the order. The availability of the documents will enable potential objectors to assess the basis for the order, to obtain an idea of what sort of objection if any is appropriate, and to understand what kind of evidence they are likely to need in order to challenge and rebut the authority's case.

Where there are objections and those objections are not withdrawn, then the Order must be submitted to the Secretary of State for confirmation (except where the Secretary of State has made the Order) and the Secretary of State must either cause a local public inquiry to be held, or must afford objectors an opportunity to be heard. The difference between the two procedures (inquiry and hearing) is that inquiries are open to the public whereas hearings are not. Both procedures are presided over by an "appointed person" commonly known as an inspector. The normal preference appears to be for a public inquiry. Where there is an objection by a local authority to an Order under the Highways Act 1980 there must be an inquiry.

Procedure

The procedure for inquiries is not defined as it is for Side Roads Order Inquiries. The procedure is subject to the provisions contained in section 250 of the Local Government Act 1972. This allows the inspector:

- to issue a summons to any person to attend and give evidence and produce any documents in his possession (on pain of summary prosecution and six months imprisonment);
- to take evidence on oath.

As a matter of practice, such witness summonses are rarely issued and evidence is not normally taken on oath.

Although there is no statutory procedure at such inquiries, the procedure being in the discretion of the inspector, the procedure is likely to be in effect the following:

> The Order-making authority shall have the right to start, which will normally involve an introductory statement by the advocate followed by the calling of evidence. Objectors will have the right to cross-examine the authority's witnesses, and the authority will have the right to re-examine.
>
> After the authority's witnesses have been called, any supporters of the authority may be given the right to present representations in support, and objectors then may cross-examine them.
>
> Objectors will have the opportunity to present their case in turn. Objectors are often encouraged to present a joint case where convenient and where several objectors are presenting what is substantially a similar objection.
>
> Each objector will have the opportunity to present an opening statement, (in person or through an advocate) then to give evidence and/or call his own witnesses. The authority will have the right to cross examine such witnesses and the objector will have the right to re-examine. After all his evidence has been called the authority will have the right to adduce rebuttal evidence and the objector will again have the right to cross-examine and the authority to re-examine. The objector will have the right to sum up his case.
>
> After the cases for all the objectors have been heard, the authority will have the opportunity to sum up the case for making the order.

The above procedure is sometimes varied by allowing for cross-examination of the authority's witnesses by objectors during the presentation of the objector's case, before the objector has called evidence, or alternatively when the rebuttal evidence is given.

The procedure is complicated in the event of an objection on the basis that the proposed route cannot be justified since the community would be better served by an alternative route. Such type of objections is rare in footpath or bridleway inquiries (a strong contrast with Side Road Order and Compulsory Purchase Inquiries), but where it does exist, provision has to be made for counter objectors, *i.e.* those who may or may not support the route proposed by the order-making authority but who in any event object to the suggested alternative route.

Site visit
The inspector will conduct a site visit shortly after he has closed the inquiry. He will normally be accompanied by a representative of the promoting authority and by at least one objector. He will not hear any representations or evidence during the site visit, but he will want to have pointed out to him features of the topography and landscape etc which have been the subject of evidence during the inquiry.

Different approaches of the highway authority and the objectors
There must be few tribunals of any kind where there is such a contrast between the roles played by the two sides as in that of a highway inquiry. The promoting authority is not only supporting the proposal but is also staging the inquiry. At the same time the promoting authority has much greater resources at its disposal and is more likely to be in a position to call expert witnesses where necessary.

This is far less frequently the case in Rights of Way Inquiries than in Side Roads Order Inquiries but there are occasions when expert witnesses will be needed on such matters as wildlife, flora and fauna and so on. Where expert witnesses are called the inspector is likely to be very much in the hands of the expert without any evidence to contradict him.

Frequently, the form of the promoting authority's case will be in the form of evidence by the authority's rights of way officer.

Preparation of cases
For the assistance of any readers preparing their own case for an inquiry, the appendix contains some suggestions as to compiling proofs of evidence.

Protection of flora and fauna
Part I of the Wildlife and Countryside Act 1981 sets out the protection afforded to wild fauna and flora that the Schedules to the Act list those birds (Sched 1), animals (Sched 5) and plants (Sched 8) given special protection.

Modifications of Orders
After an Order has been made, the rules concerning the making and confirmation of Orders normally allow for the modification of the order by the Secretary of State where the Secretary of State is the confirming authority. However modifications may not ordinarily be made where they would affect land not affected by the original order (under para (3) of Sched 6 of the Highways Act and para 8 of Sched 15 to the Wildlife and Countryside Act 1981) or, in the case of modification Orders, to show a way not shown in the Order or to exclude any way shown in the original Order, or to show a highway as being of one description when it was shown in the original Order as being a highway of another description (paragraph 8 of Schedule 15 to the Wildlife and Countryside Act 1981).

Modifications should therefore normally be restricted to matters of detail and Circular No 2/93 contains the following:

> "Authorities may care to note that the Secretaries of State do not regard the power of modification vested in them as available to make good orders which would otherwise be incapable of confirmation because they are defective in a matter of substance. The Secretaries of State, in their consideration of orders, normally disregard errors or defects of a minor nature provided they do not, in their view, prejudice the interests of any person, render the order misleading in its purpose or appear to result in incorrect information being recorded on the definitive map. Nonetheless care should be taken in drafting orders to ensure that they are correct and free from errors and defects, to reduce the possibility of their validity being challenged at a later stage in the procedure."

After the Inquiry
The Secretary of State or person appointed by the Secretary of State or other relevant authority will be required to publish the result of the Inquiry and any Order which is made or confirmed as the result of the decision. There is provision for service of the notice of confirmation on relevant owners, local authorities and those persons required to be served with the original Order. (See *e.g.* Sched 15 of the Wildlife and Countryside Act 1981.)

There may be a power of statutory review of any Order which is made as the result of the Inquiry. In relation to Orders made under the Highways Act, the provisions for statutory review are contained in Schedule 2 to the Act.

Under the Highways Act
After publication of the decision, any person who is aggrieved by the (scheme or) Order in question and desires to question the validity of it or any provision contained in it on the ground that

- it is not within the powers of the Highways Act; or
- that any requirement of the Highways Act or regulations made under it have not been complied with,

he may apply to the High Court for review of the Order.

Under the Wildlife and Countryside Act 1981
A procedure for review of the Order is available which is similar to that under the Highways Act.

Appendix

Preparation for Inquiries

Proofs of evidence
Both the authority and the objectors will need to produce proofs of evidence for use at the inquiry. A proof is simply a written statement of evidence to be given at the Inquiry which may either be read out or taken as read. (Sometimes summaries are accepted by way of proof.) This is by far the most satisfactory way to produce evidence and many inspectors will insist on it. Some objectors find this worrying, but it is in many ways a blessing since it makes people consider what they really want to say to the Inquiry. In drafting proofs of evidence, the following thoughts may be of help.

The statutory criteria
The inspector will be approaching the inquiry by asking himself "On what issues do I have to be satisfied to persuade me to confirm (or recommend confirmation of) the order?" If the authority or the objectors do not concentrate on the answer to this question then a great deal of time is likely to be wasted.

Let us take as an example a section 119 public path diversion Order. Section 119 states:

> "(6) The Secretary of State shall not confirm a public path diversion order ... unless he ... [is] satisfied that the diversion to be affected by it is expedient [in the interests of the owner lessee or occupier of land crossed by the path or way or of the public] ... and that it is expedient to confirm the order having regard to the effect which–
>
> (a) the diversion would have on public enjoyment of the path or way as a whole;
> (b) the coming into operation of the order would have as respects other land served by the existing public rights of way, and
> (c) any new public right of way created by the order would have as respects the land over which the right is so created and any land held with it
>
> so, however that for the purposes of paragraphs (b) and (c) above the Secretary of State or, as the case may be, the council shall take into account the provisions as to compensation referred to in subsection (5)(a) above."

Clearly any case to be put before the inspector at an inquiry needs to focus on the criteria appearing in this section. Any inspector would be greatly helped to see how the case for the authority or an objector works if a statement of case proof of evidence contained headings such as "The effect which the diversion would have on public enjoyment of the path [or way] as a whole." If this is done it becomes abundantly clear what the party or witness is seeking to persuade him of.

It also makes it clear to the inspector that the person who presents a proof in such form has given thought to the matters at issue and is not simply using the inquiry to air his grievances. An inspector is surely likely to give more weight to a proof set out in this way.

Setting out the proof
Division of the proof into separate sections, with subject headings and sub-headings often helps to make clear the way in which the witness puts his case. It also helps the inspector and other participants at the inquiry if they want to refer back to particular points made on a certain issue.

Informing the Inspector
For both sides the objective should be to inform the inspector. The inspector will on his site visit see for himself many of the physical features which are relevant to the issues. However a good deal of thought needs to be given by both sides to the things which he will not see. These include the conditions which are likely to arise at times of year and in conditions other than those pertaining when the inspector makes his visit.

How prone are sites to flooding?

How prone is a location to the formation of ice?

How likely is it that equestrian traffic at particular locations will result in mud in wet weather?

How safe is the proposed path or way?

Is it likely to be used by children? Clearly the combination of horses and children can give rise to danger.

Does the proposed path or way join a main road? If so what are the safety considerations at that location?

What is visibility like?

Is the area prone to fog?

Does the path or way come down a hill at the point of the junction, and if so is that likely to cause problems for equestrians? If so, could the junction easily be re-sited at a better location?

Would it not be better to provide a bridge or subway?

What would be the cost of a bridge or subway?

Are there circular routes or rides?

Are there user groups in the area?

Will the proposed way or path be used mainly by long distance walkers or local residents taking their dog for a walk?

The above issues involve to a greater or lesser extent information which the inspector cannot see with his own eyes. The only way he is going to get that information is if the parties on both sides attempt to put themselves in his shoes and think about what information he will and will not have. This exercise requires some imagination and thought and there can be little doubt that inadequacy of presentation at inquiries frequently results from parties on both sides failing to carry it out fully. Objectors, who may have no experience whatsoever of public inquiries, frequently find themselves assuming that an inspector will know something which on reflection he is extremely unlikely to know if he comes from the other side of the country or even the county.

Brevity
If a point can be made briefly it tends to be more effectively made than if it is buried in a mass of verbiage. It is very important that the witness thinks carefully about which points go to the issues in the inquiry and relates the text of the proof to those issues in turn. If a proof ranges in an ambling way over a series of subjects, it makes the impression that the witness has not taken an overall view of the issues.

Evidential aids
Photographs of individual locations, perhaps showing particular conditions, maps, and statistical tables can often tell a story vividly and graphically and far more effectively than many pages of text.

Statement of Case
In addition to proofs of evidence a Statement of Case may be prepared. A Statement of Case is a summary of the argument and facts put forward by the party concerned. From the objector's side a Statement of Case may only be called for in the more complex cases, unless expressly required by the Inspector. It is particularly useful where a party is calling more than one witness. In the Statement of Case the evidence of the witnesses can be related to each other and it is shown how they fit into the case as a whole.

Index